Reflecting on Literacy in Educat

Literacy has become central to debates on policy and practice in education in the UK and other English-speaking countries. This book introduces teachers and tutors to ways of thinking about literacy, and its place in education, from the different perspectives of history, politics, sociology, psychology and curricular theory.

Reflecting on Literacy in Education discusses key ideas, and relates practical and policy concerns to an understanding of theoretical issues. Concise and accessible, it provides suggestions for further reading and connects with key aspects of the experience of professionals and students alike, including their own writing, reading and researching.

Peter Hannon is currently Professor of Education at the University of Sheffield where he has directed research projects in parental involvement, family literacy and pre-school intervention. He has taught several Masters' courses, including the University of Sheffield distance education MEd in Literacy and is also the author of *Literacy, Home and School* (Falmer, 1995).

Master Classes in Education Series

Series Editors: John Head, School of Education, King's College, University of London, and Ruth Merttens, School of Teaching Studies, University of North London.

Working with Adolescents: Constructing Identity
John Head *King's College, University of London*

Testing: Friend or Foe? The Theory and Practice of Assessment and Testing
Paul Black *King's College, University of London*

Doing Research/Reading Research: A Mode of Interrogation for Education
Andrew Brown and Paul Dowling *both of the Institute of Education, University of London*

Educating the Other: Gender, Power and Schooling
Carrie Paechter *School of Education, The Open University*

Reflecting on School Management
Anne Gold and Jennifer Evans *both of the Institute of Education, University of London*

School Effectiveness: Fracturing the Discourse
Louise Morley *University of Sussex* and Naz Rassool *University of Reading*

Curriculum: Construction and Critique
Alistair Ross *University of North London*

Master Classes in Education Series

Reflecting on Literacy in Education

Peter Hannon

First Published 2000
by RoutledgeFalmer
11 New Fetter Lane, London EC4P 4EE

Simultaneously published in the USA and Canada by RoutledgeFalmer
29 West 35th Street, New York, NY 10001

RoutledgeFalmer is an imprint of the Taylor and Francis Group

© 2000 Peter Hannon

Typeset in Sabon by J&L Composition Ltd, Filey, North Yorkshire
Printed and bound in Great Britain by TJ International Ltd, Padstow, Cornwall

British Library Cataloguing in Publication Data
A catalogue record for this book is available from the British Library

Library of Congress Cataloging in Publication Data
A catalog record for this book has been requested

ISBN 0–750–70832–8 (hbk)
ISBN 0–750–70831–X (pbk)

Contents

Series Editor's Preface

It has become a feature of our times that an initial qualification is no longer seen to be adequate for life-long work within a profession and programmes of professional development are needed. Nowhere is the need more clear than with respect to education, where changes in the national schooling and assessment system, combined with changes in the social and economic context, have transformed our professional lives.

The series, *Master Classes in Education*, is intended to address the needs of professional development, essentially at the level of taught Masters' degrees. Although aimed primarily at teachers and lecturers, it is envisaged that the books will appeal to a wider readership, including those involved in professional educational management, health promotion and youth work. For some, the texts will serve to update their knowledge. For others, they may facilitate career reorientation by introducing, in an accessible form, new areas of expertise or knowledge.

The books are overtly pedagogical, providing a clear track through the topic by means of which it is possible to gain a sound grasp of the whole field. Each book familiarises the reader with the vocabulary and the terms of discussion, and provides a concise overview of recent research and current debates in the area. While it is obviously not possible to deal with every aspect in depth, a professional who has read the book should feel confident that they have covered the major areas of content, and discussed the different issues at stake. The books are also intended to convey a sense of the future direction of the subject and its points of growth or change.

In each subject area the reader is introduced to different perspectives and to a variety of readings of the subject under consideration. Some of the readings may conflict, others may be compatible but distant. Different perspectives may well give rise to different lexicons and different bibliographies, and the reader is always alerted to these differences. The variety of frameworks within which each topic can be constructed is then a further source of reflective analysis.

The authors in this series have been carefully selected. Each person is an experienced professional, who has worked in that area of education as a practitioner and also addressed the subject as a researcher and theoretician. Drawing upon both pragmatic and theoretical aspects of their experience, they are able to take a reflective view while preserving a sense of what occurs, and what is possible, at the level of practice.

Reflecting on Literacy in Education

There are few debates in education which are as politically polarised as those on the subject of literacy. And there are few topics which are as guaranteed to elicit a strong opinion from almost any teacher, lecturer, parent or politician. Teaching children to read, and the allegedly falling standards of student literacy, are both subjects about which almost everyone has a theory.

Peter Hannon enters these troubled areas without apparent trepidation. He writes neither as a polemicist for one side in the debate nor as an apologist for the other. Instead, he sets out to inform and to teach. He provides us with a careful track through the terrain in order that, better informed and with a more comprehensive understanding, we may be able to decide our own position within this complex field, and thus to argue our own case. But what a muddy terrain the field itself turns out to be! The complexity of the arguments, the ways in which a proposition in one dimension is related to an apparently separate set of ideas in another, and the overall confusion of theory and fact, in other circumstances would be daunting.

Professor Hannon adopts a camly logical approach. He starts be setting out the terms and the context of current debating points, and by stating his own beliefs that:

- Literacy is really important in education and is fundamental to political aspirations and to contemporary human culture.
- Educational research is an important means of improving our understanding of literature and the practice of teaching it.
- There is a literacy problem, in Britain and in comparable countries – the literacy levels of young people are probably inadequate for the social and economic demands now facing them.

The book continues in a clear and unambiguous fashion, relating literacy to socio-economic inequality, and explaining why literacy can therefore be described as fundamental.

The first part of the book takes the reader through a concise yet pertinent history of the subject. In contrast to some historical discussions, Peter Hannon is concerned to relate our understanding of the history of literacy to our sense of its future. The point, he feels, about understanding where we have come from, is to enable a better comprehension of where literacy is going to, or, in this case, the likely directions in which technological as well as political innovations will take us. This chapter relates closely to the next, where the whole question of whether to adopt a unitary or pluralist approach to literacy (or literacies) is reviewed in detail. The middle sections of the book enable the reader to step back and review the various and interconnecting theories within the field. Theories of teaching, learning and the development of literacy are outlined, and their relationships to the political imperatives of the times are discussed. The final part of the book leads the reader, through a sustained consideration of the place of research in the field, towards an understanding of literacy in their own professional development.

This book presents, as the title suggests, a reflective account of the subject. When the topic is one which is evidently not only riven by ideological positionings, but also divided by political as well as educational debate, it becomes all the more important that we have a cool and considered review of the whole field. Peter Hannon provides us with just such a text. The book is both fair to all sides and thorough, detailed and comprehensive. However, it should not be imagined that this cool, reflective and careful account indicates an academic distance from, or a lack of passion about, the very real issues of social inequality and economic disadvantage which are at stake here. The author conveys to us his sense of urgency and concern about these things, stating at the very outset that 'there are huge variations in literacy levels within society which, even if they do not wholly explain social inequalities, are a serious impediment to reducing inequality'. It is the passionate conviction that education can and should address itself to the elimination of this inequality in literacy levels that underpins every page in this book.

Ruth Merttens
Joint Series Editor

Preface

My aim in this book is to share some reflections on literacy in education and ways of researching it to readers who are new to study in this field. The particular readers I have in mind are practitioners studying on Masters' or other advanced courses in education. They could be teachers in primary or secondary schools, adult educators, preschool educators or other education professionals. Some may be intending to make a sustained study in literacy – for example, by taking an MEd in Literacy which includes a dissertation on a literacy topic – and for them I hope to provide some pathways into a larger landscape. For others, literacy may be only one among several interests, and for them I aim to provide an overview of that landscape before they turn elsewhere. I hope, of course, that outside the intended readership there may be others who will find something of interest. Literacy is increasingly a topic in its own right in courses in education, culture and communication studies.

I do not claim to offer an impartial guide to the whole field of literacy in education. This book is partial, not only because it is short and inevitably selective but, more fundamentally, because it reflects one writer's values, beliefs and experience. Let me explain what these are at the outset so that readers can judge what they might gain by going further.

A basic value for me is that literacy really is important in education – not the most important thing but important enough to be a central concern for many teachers and tutors. Another value is that I am committed to educational research as one means of improving our understanding of literacy and the practice of teaching it. I believe that if educational research is to affect practice, practitioners have to find it intelligible and relevant. For that to occur, researcher–practitioner dialogue is essential. Researchers have to engage critically with practice and communicate their research findings clearly to practitioners. But it is equally important for practitioners to engage critically with research which means them having time, space and encouragement to study research throughout their careers. Where possible practitioners should at some point in their careers be researchers themselves (although that does not mean that practitioners need constantly to be researching all of their practice themselves or that all researchers need be practitioners).

My values and beliefs have been shaped by experience of research in the field of literacy – particularly in the areas of early literacy development and the home–school interface. This has meant a sustained and – for me – rewarding dialogue with many practitioners. I have come to appreciate different research methods for answering different research questions in different circumstances. I have also been a tutor, supervisor and university teacher of students – almost all of them practitioners – engaging with research or undertaking it themselves. That is the experience I draw on in introducing some issues in the field, putting forward arguments on others, and making suggestions about carrying out research in professional contexts.

Since 1992 I have been fortunate to work with a group of colleagues at the University of Sheffield in devising and teaching a distance learning Master's course in Literacy and, more recently, developing a Literacy PhD Programme. I have learned an enormous amount from past and present colleagues – particularly Ann Finlay, Geoff Lindsay, Elaine Millard, Cathy Nutbrown and Jo Weinberger – whose individual research and other contributions to the literacy field are widely recognised. I do not presume to write much about topics where they are more expert but I mention their work and point readers to their publications. My colleagues deserve credit for aspects of this book which may prove valuable although I cannot, unfortunately, blame them or anyone else for its defects.

It is our teaching at Sheffield which has given me the opportunity for dialogue with committed and questioning students from across the UK and other countries who teach literacy in a wide range of contexts including the preschool sector, schools, adult education and in various communities. I have learned a great deal from that dialogue and see this book as a way of putting some of it into writing.

The book is structured around my response to some basic questions. What is literacy and why is it now seen as so important? What has been its history and what might be its future? Is there more than one kind of literacy? How can we understand the development of literacy in individuals? How should it be taught? How can we research literacy in education? What part does literacy play in the professional development of teachers, tutors and other readers of this book? The way in which I respond to these questions, and my choice and framing of the questions, reflect my learning experiences as a researcher and university teacher. I acknowledge that others – even in similar positions – might give priority to different questions and answers but we need difference and debate. If in some areas I manage only to give readers something to disagree with, I may still have succeeded in playing a part in the development of our collective thinking.

Chapter 1 considers how literacy is fundamental to human culture today and therefore why it is fundamental to the aims and the processes of education. I restate and develop some ideas first put forward in an earlier book, *Literacy, Home and School* (Hannon, 1995). Chapter 2 takes a step back in order to gain a fuller view of how literacy has changed in the five millennia since it entered human history and how it continues to change as we enter the new millennium. Chapter 3 considers a fundamental issue about which there are contrasting views from different research perspectives, namely whether there is one thing which can be called literacy or whether there are many literacies. All literacy teaching rests on some kind of theory of how it develops in children and adults; Chapter 4 surveys some current theories. This leads, in Chapter 5, to issues of how literacy is taught – to adults as well as to children – and the value of different teaching methods.

The final chapters shift the focus to the readers of the book and I venture some suggestions about how, if they are studying on courses, readers can find out about research, carry out research themselves, read about it and write about it. Thus in Chapter 6, I ask 'How can we research literacy in education?' and I advocate a multidisciplinary approach which includes methods likely to be used by teacher-researchers studying at Master's or doctorate level. In Chapter 7 I invite readers, particularly teachers, to consider the place of literacy not only in the lives of those they teach but also in their own development especially in relation to their own professional development, study and research. The concluding Chapter 8 draws together ideas about literacy teaching, literacy research and professional development into a vision of how these may be more fruitfully linked in the future.

Because the book is introductory, and one of the RoutledgeFalmer *Master Classes in Education* series, I have suggested some books for each chapter to enable readers to follow up particular topics in more depth.

Reflecting on the range of literacy studies in recent years from which I could select for these chapters it seemed to me that not only was there a huge amount of work but also it now amounts to a *rethinking* of answers to familiar questions. We not only have more information about key issues but also new ways of thinking about some of them. Literacy is being rethought from many different research perspectives. Never before has it been so prominent in educational debates across the world and never before has it received so much attention from researchers in disciplines such as psychology, sociology, linguistics, history and politics. The field of literacy research cannot be claimed as the sole province of any of these traditional disciplines. Therefore the book moves across disciplinary boundaries in an attempt to provide snapshots, from different perspectives, of literacy in education. There are many unresolved issues in literacy research and theory. As I tend to find polarities such as 'phonics versus real books' or 'quantitative versus qualitative research' unhelpful I try to suggest ways in which views can be reconciled. Elsewhere all one can do is juxtapose different views.

The title of this book, *Reflecting on Literacy in Education*, is not meant to suggest that my own reflections on these questions are of any special significance but to point out that the work of many researchers and theorists is giving us fresh ways of thinking about familiar topics. It is also intended to point out that practitioners, too, can reflect on literacy in education through their study, research and a fuller participation in the educational community.

Chapter 1

Literacy Is Fundamental

Overview

Much is heard these days of a literacy crisis. Although talk of crisis may be exaggerated for political purposes it is still worth trying to identify the nature of current literacy problems. They relate to ever increasing literacy demands in society and to the uneven distribution of literacy competence in the population. Literacy has been, and continues to be, fundamental to political aspirations and to contemporary human culture. It is therefore fundamental to education. Current literacy policy development in England can be reviewed in this context.

A Literacy Crisis?

Why do we hear so much about literacy in education these days? Ten or twenty years ago the term had very limited currency and was used mainly in relation to adult illiteracy. Now it figures daily in both professional and popular discourse about schools and education. In 1998 the government in England declared a Year of Reading and launched a National Literacy Strategy.

Underlying the discourse is anxiety – not only in the UK but in other countries around the world. It is perhaps understandable in those countries where many adults are classed as illiterate and primary education is not yet universal. Economic progress, improvements in health and perhaps political development could be seen in such countries as requiring improved literacy and, even though United Nations statistics indicate that more people in the world, and a higher than ever proportion of the world's population, are literate, anxiety about the rate of improvement is understandable. But how can the anxiety be explained in long-industrialised countries where there has been universal primary education for several generations? In these 'developed' countries there is concern about a minority of illiterate adults and there are complaints about the inadequacy of workforce literacy skills needed for competition in international markets. This is often accompanied by controversy about how schools should teach literacy.

In 1997 a government White Paper in England asserted that 'our performance in literacy is behind a number of comparable English-speaking countries' and 'standards of literacy have not changed significantly between the end of the war and the early 1990s' (Department for Education and Employment (DfEE), 1997, p. 19). In the United States, Steven Pinker, a prominent researcher in language and professor at the Massachusetts Institute of Technology, asserted: 'We are turning into a nation of illiterates, the victims of misguided ideas about the nature of reading and how to teach it' (Pinker, 1998, pp. ix–x). Can things be so bad? If there is a crisis, what exactly is its nature? What are the likely causes, what are the likely remedies, and how well do proposed remedies relate to causes?

We should be cautious about accepting crisis talk at face value. If politicians are to the fore in drawing attention to a 'crisis', defining its nature and proposing remedies, a certain amount of scepticism is advisable. One has to be alert, for example, to the possibility that it may be in the interests of some groups in society if the 'literacy crisis' diverts attention from other problems of social order, economic decline, unemployment or educational provision (or if it can be presented as the root cause of such problems). Another possibility is that the vocabulary of literacy is being appropriated for ideological purposes in order to disguise or justify processes of exclusion in society. If certain social groups are oppressed and if they are also largely illiterate (according to some concept of 'literacy') it may be convenient to explain their position as being *the result* of illiteracy. This is a more comforting explanation for social ills than accounts in terms, say, of racism, market forces or the needs of the rich. In so far as illiteracy serves as a justification for injustice, it may even be in the interests of ruling groups in society to perpetuate illiteracy in certain groups. This can be done by lower resourcing of literacy teaching (e.g. reduced funding for books, unfavourable teacher–pupil ratios). There can be overly rigid definitions of what is to count as literacy and biased or narrow forms of assessment. As Denny Taylor (1997) has argued,

> Race, gender and socioeconomic status are all factors that critically affect whose 'literacy' counts. There seems to be a limit to how much success there is to go around, and not all types of knowledge or ways of knowing are recognized. (Taylor, 1997, p. 2)

In some discourse, the term 'illiterate' can serve as a substitute for 'unemployed', 'poor', 'black' or 'working class'. The definition of illiteracy can be narrowed or widened as convenient. For example, in the United States, illiteracy is sometimes equated with 'high school drop out' thereby implying that a very large group of people face the difficulties which ought perhaps to be ascribed to only a few. To reinforce the point, there can be attempts to ameliorate the circumstances of such groups by attempts to raise literacy levels which do not improve matters much because they do not address the real problem. Freire (1972) provided a blunt commentary on this.

> Merely teaching men to read and write does not work miracles; if there are not enough jobs for men able to work, teaching more men to read and write will not create them. (Freire, 1972, p. 25)

The United Nations was led to proclaim 1990 as 'International Literacy Year' on the grounds that illiteracy was linked to poverty, underdevelopment, child health and economic, social and cultural exclusion (UNESCO, 1988). These views invite the metaphor of illiteracy as disease – something to be eradicated. The author of a recent UK report on basic skills (Working Group on Post-School Basic Skills, 1999) has referred in a radio interview to adults with limited literacy skills as having a 'mental disability' (Moser, 1999). Yet the fullest possible literacy will not be sufficient to bring about the changes sought unless there are also changes in other determining factors. Graff (1979) has shown that there is little historical justification for supposing that in the past increased literacy led to (rather than was merely associated with) economic progress. In the future, literacy may, at best, be a necessary condition for certain kinds of development; it cannot possibly be a sufficient condition.

In the United States, there has emerged a 'family literacy' rhetoric (Hannon, 1999) in which poverty and unemployment are represented as problems caused by a 'cycle' of low literacy levels in certain communities. Elsa Auerbach has commented,

> Suggesting that enhanced family literacy interactions will break the cycle of poverty or compensate for problems facing the educational system only reinforces the ideology that blames poor people for their own problems and leaves social inequities intact. (Auerbach, 1995, p. 23)

Nevertheless, the possibility – likelihood, even – that there is an element of political cynicism in claims about a literacy crisis does not mean that there is no problem. The challenge is to clarify the nature and extent of the problem.

The Nature of the Literacy Problem

I wish to argue that there is a literacy problem in Britain and comparable countries and that it has two interrelated aspects. First, the literacy levels of some young people are probably inadequate for the social and economic demands now facing them. Second, there are huge variations in literacy levels within society which, even if they do not wholly explain social inequalities, are a serious impediment to reducing inequality.

The literacy levels of school leavers has been a recurrent issue of controversy. Almost a generation ago, in 1972, in England, it led the government to set up the Bullock Committee to enquire into standards and methods of teaching. The committee received evidence from many people who believed standards of literacy had fallen but it pointed out that similar complaints could be found fifty years previously in the Newbolt Report of 1921 where one employer had stated that 'teaching of English in present day schools produces a very limited command of the English language' (Department of Education and Science (DES), 1975, p. 3). The Bullock Report, although widely acclaimed by professionals in education and highly influential, did not allay anxieties for long. By the end of the 1980s the controversy had surfaced again and further reports were required (DES, 1990;

Cato and Whetton, 1991). Parallel developments occurred in other industrialised countries.

Determining the literacy level of children in school, and judging whether it is rising or falling, is not an easy matter but studies which have been carried out suggest there is no evidence in Britain that the level has fallen since the 1940s (Brooks et al., 1996; Hurry, 1999). Neither does it appear to have risen, however, and that may be cause for concern given that the literacy demands of work and society have probably increased in that period. Certainly there are far fewer jobs available now for school leavers with low literacy competence. Even if the day-to-day requirements of some jobs are not very demanding, they do not stay the same for long and the process of retraining often makes literacy demands. In literacy, as in many other areas of life, it is doubtful whether the standards of the late 1940s can be considered adequate for the new century.

Many governments claim that retaining their economic position in the global economy means having a skilled, well-educated (and therefore highly literate) workforce. Workers unable to meet these demands will be unemployed and therefore socially excluded. It is the literacy level of this group which could be said to constitute a problem. In 1988 the European Commission argued that the 'persistence of illiteracy in industrialised countries' of the Community was 'a worrying social problem concerning a large number of the working population' (Commission of the European Communities, 1988). Against the background of attempts by the Community to establish itself as a competitive industrial and trading bloc, the Commission expressed concern about the 'social cost of illiteracy in our societies, in terms of manpower which can only be retrained with difficulty, in terms of unused potential'. An action research programme in 'the prevention and combating of illiteracy' was launched.

Yet the links between economic development and levels of literacy are far from clear as Peter Robinson (1997) has pointed out.

> according to World Bank data, the two most successful small Asian economies, Singapore and Hong Kong, had in 1985 adult illiteracy rates of 14 and 12 per cent respectively, rising to 20 per cent for women. So their impressive economic progress does not appear to have been hampered by levels of adult illiteracy significantly higher than in the advanced industrial economies where functional illiteracy rates are typically less than 1 per cent. (Robinson, 1997, p. 19)

Robinson also points out that the annual Skills Needs Survey by the Department for Education and Employment shows only 4 per cent of employers reporting that their business objectives were being hampered by a lack of literacy and numeracy among their employees. Employers were much more concerned about motivation and lack of skills in management, information and general communication.

Nevertheless, adults with literacy difficulties do constitute a small but significant minority in Britain and comparable societies. Exact numbers are difficult to determine since there are methodological problems in defining illiteracy and in surveying and assessing adults' competence. Research in the United States has sought to determine levels of literacy in terms of performance criteria. The National Adult Literacy Survey sampled around 13,600 adults and distinguished five levels of literacy (Kirsch et al., 1993). It found that almost a quarter had skills in the lowest level of proficiencies and were unable to perform 'quite limited' reading and writing tasks. The study also showed a huge variation in literacy skills related to quality of life and employment opportunities.

Testing adults may not be the best way to determine literacy levels since literacy ability is a relative concept and what matters is the individual's ability to cope with the demands they experience in society. The alternative is to use adults' self-reports of literacy difficulties (although that is open to criticism on the grounds that it relies on individuals' own judgements about their abilities and various factors such as their job, their aspirations or their understanding of the interview questions could lead to either an over-estimate or an under-estimate of 'true' literacy levels).

The approach of simply asking adults whether they have had difficulties with reading or writing since leaving school was taken in Britain in the fourth National Child Development Study follow-up study when a national sample of over 12,500 23-year-olds was interviewed (Adult Literacy and Basic Skills Unit (ALBSU), 1987). Around 10 per cent of the adults reported difficulties with reading, writing or spelling. Of these, about half had difficulties just with writing (including spelling) but not with reading; the others had difficulties with both. Fewer than one in ten of those with difficulties had attended any kind of adult literacy course. Although some had had literacy difficulties at school and were in manual jobs, it is interesting that a significant number had not received any special help in school and were in non-manual jobs. In other words, the 'illiterate' on this definition did not conform to any easily identified stereotype. Although about a quarter reported that their literacy difficulties were in some way work-related, for most they were encountered in a wide range of contexts.

These findings were replicated in a later British study of a nationally representative sample of 1,650 21-year-olds (Ekinsmyth and Bynner, 1994). The pattern of self-reported difficulties appears to be the same as in the 1987 study but this study also assessed the young people's performance on a set of tasks. It found that 5 per cent could not find a restaurant address from the Yellow Pages, 24 per cent could not locate basic information in a video recorder manual, and 48 per cent could not read advice about how to help someone suffering from hypothermia. Literacy scores based on such tasks were strongly related to family background, school attainment and employment history. The authors concluded,

> A picture emerges of the person lacking basic skills as being marginalised first in education and then in the peripheral unskilled regions of the labour market, typically with long spells of unemployment. (Ekinsmyth and Bynner, 1994, p. 55)

In 1999 a working group chaired by Claus Moser claimed that 7 million adults in England, one in five of the adult population, was functionally illiterate (Working Group on Post-School Basic Skills, 1999, p. 8). The evidence quoted was that this proportion of adults, given the alphabetical index to the Yellow Pages, could not locate the page reference for plumbers. The working group proposed a National Strategy with increased opportunities for adult learners, a basic skill curriculum, a new sytem of qualifications, teacher training, inspection of courses, more use of information technology, and greatly increased funding for this area of education.

The Moser recommendations are premised on a very high – perhaps an implausibly high – estimate of the prevalence of illiteracy in England. However, even if one accepts the figure of 7 million adults, it could still be argued that if there is a problem concerning literacy levels it is not one of generally low levels (however defined) in the population as a whole so much as a problem of a significant group within the population. There might be arguments about whether it is 5, 10, 15 or 20 per cent of the population but there is a high degree of consensus that the problem of standards is not general but specific to a minority. This is borne out by a study by Brooks et al. (1996) which found that, in comparison with other countries, there was a long 'tail' of low scoring 9-year-olds in England and Wales on a reading test used in an international study.

What is known about the group of low attainers? Brooks et al. (1996) found that boys were more likely than girls to have low reading scores (a difference of four points on a standardised scores) but an even stronger association was found with low family income (a nine-point difference, where low family income was defined in terms of entitlement to free school meals). This accords with evidence going back many years from National Child Development Study surveys of children aged 7, 11 and 14 which have shown wide and growing differences between children from different social backgrounds (Davie et al., 1972; Fogelman and Goldstein, 1976; Wedge and Prosser, 1973). At age 11 children from the most disadvantaged 6 per cent of households were an average of three-and-a-half years behind others in reading test scores (Wedge and Prosser, 1973).

In summary, there would appear to be a literacy problem in terms of standards in schools which have not risen as one might have expected over the last half century but, importantly, that this problem relates to a sub-group of the population.

The Politics of Literacy

Literacy is often associated with radical political goals – to do with demands for democratic rights and power. The fact that written language can be such a powerful tool means that the question of who should be able to use it, and what they should use it for, has always been deeply political. The historical trend in most societies has been for literacy to spread from more powerful groups to the rest of the population. The least powerful are the last to become literate, and the kind of literacy they are expected to acquire may not extend to all uses of written language.

It has been argued that literacy is essential for political freedom (a 'necessary condition for liberty' to use George Bernard Shaw's phrase), for access to political ideas, and for the level of organisation needed to bring about political change.

However, here too what matters is not literacy in itself but its place in a wider political education. Increased literacy cannot be a goal in itself. Neither is it a guarantee of economic, political or personal progress. It can even make it easier to control people – as has been argued by Neil Postman (1970).

> It is probably true that in a highly complex society, one cannot be governed unless he can read forms, regulations, notices, catalogues, road signs, and the like. Thus, some minimal reading skill is necesary if you are to be a 'good citizen', but 'good citizen' here means one who can follow the instructions of those who govern him. If you cannot read, you cannot be an obedient citizen. You are also a good citizen if you are an enthusiastic consumer. And so, some minimal reading competence is required if you are going to develop a keen interest in all the products that it is necessary for you to buy. If you do not read, you will be a relatively poor market. In order to be a good and loyal citizen, it is also necessary for you to believe in the myths and superstitions of your society. Therefore, a certain minimal reading skill is needed so that you can learn what these are, or have them reinforced. (Postman, 1970, p. 246)

We should be wary of promoting literacy as if it were self-evidently an end in itself. It is rather a means by which learners can reach goals which they may value for themselves or their children.

Brian Street (1984) has proposed what he calls an 'ideological' model of literacy and he has argued that the meaning of literacy cannot be separated from the social institutions in which it is practised or the social processes whereby practitioners acquire it.

> The actual examples of literacy in different societies that are available to us suggest that it is more often 'restrictive' and hegemonic, and concerned with instilling discipline and exercising social order. (Street, 1984, p. 4)

In similar vein, James Gee (1996) has argued,

> The most striking continuity in the history of literacy is the way in which literacy has been used, in age after age, to solidify the social hierarchy, empower elites, and ensure that people lower on the the hierarchy accept the values, norms, and beliefs of the elites, even when it is not in their self-interest or group interest to do so. (Gee, 1996, p. 36)

It is not possible here to attempt to disentangle everything which makes literacy such a political issue. One has to take care to avoid uncritical formulations of what are problems and what are solutions. Literacy does have a potential for both oppression and liberation. The view taken by many educators – and an assumption underlying this book – is that it is worth trying to provide the maximum number of children and adults with the opportunity to use written language as fully as possible for purposes they value. It cannot be assumed that, by itself, the ability to participate in any particular literacy activity, is sufficient to secure any specific political goal. All that education can hope to achieve is to provide learners with options to exercise if they choose.

Literacy in Education

Literacy is not only one of the principal goals of education but also one of the principal means by which it is carried out. Virtually all schooling, after the first year or two, assumes pupil literacy. This is particularly so to the extent that children are expected to work independently of teachers, for that requires them to read work sheets, written directions, reference materials, and so on. Many schools are anxious to encourage this pattern of pupil learning from the earliest possible stage – which means establishing literacy as soon as possible after school entry. The corollary is that children who find reading and writing difficult are disadvantaged in *all* areas of the curriculum.

The intellectual consequences of being able to read have been explored by Margaret Donaldson (1978). She has argued that 'the early mastery of reading is even more important than it is commonly taken to be' because, from the standpoint of psychological theory, children's thinking develops when something gives them pause and they have to consider more than one possibility. She suggests that,

> the lasting character of the print means that there is time to stop and think, so that the child has a chance to consider possibilities – a chance of a kind which he may never have had before. (Donaldson, 1978, p. 95)

There may well be other ways in which this kind of thinking could be developed but literacy is clearly one, very powerful, way.

At a deeper level, literacy is fundamental to education because the ability to use written language to derive and convey meaning is fundamental to contemporary culture and thinking. The teaching of literacy is about one generation equipping the next with a powerful cultural tool. Written language enables members of a culture to communicate without meeting; to express and explore their experience; to store information, ideas and knowledge; to extend their memory and thinking; and, increasingly nowadays, to control computer-based processes.

Communication between people who do not meet – and perhaps never could meet – is one of the most obvious uses for written language. This means, for example, at a mundane level, that parents can send a note to school to explain a child's absence or, at a more profound level, that a single author's work can reach millions of readers. The writers and readers who are in communication may know each other or they may be complete strangers, widely separated by distance and time. They may even be separated by many generations. The written language may be used for a letter, a financial transaction, a vehicle repair manual, a public record, a news report, a legal statute, a novel, a recipe, or a philosophical argument. Literacy means being able to make fuller use of such shared cultural resources and being able to interact more fully with an enormous range of other people.

Writers can also use written language to communicate with themselves. They may do so simply as an aid to memory when, for example, writing a shopping list or noting appointments in a diary. They are in effect writing to themselves in the future. But it can go further when authors seek to organise their thoughts by writing them out, reading them (almost as if they were someone else's), reviewing, and then revising them. We shall return to this in Chapter 7, 'Literacy in Professional Development'.

Thus literacy means much more than just decoding letter–sound correspondences in reading or forming letters and spelling correctly in writing (vital though these skills are). No one reads simply to decode or writes simply to form letters. It is fundamentally a matter of understanding others' meanings or communicating meaningfully with them rather than exercising specific perceptual and motor skills.

A thought experiment demonstrates the fundamental importance of literacy. Imagine becoming, for some reason, quite unable to read or write but still having to live in a literate culture. What would it mean? For most readers of this book it would mean giving up their present employment, a massive loss of independence, and reliance on family, friends and others to accomplish the simplest tasks of everyday life. It would mean being denied all the uses of literacy discussed so far. The far reaching implications of such a personal disaster are a further measure of the value of literacy.

It is not just readers drawn from a rather narrow, highly educated section of society, who value literacy. Anyone in an industrialised society who has difficulties in reading or writing immediately faces many other problems. There is the fear of being stigmatised as illiterate – which means that many go to considerable lengths to disguise their inability to use written language ('I haven't got my glasses' or 'I haven't got a pencil'). One could argue that this is simple prejudice – to be resisted like other kinds based on race, gender or disability – but illiteracy by itself and without any other social process means exclusion from many aspects of the culture whether it be reading books, football results, TV listings, food packaging or filling in simple forms and sending greetings cards. Job opportunities (and even the confidence to seek employment) are extremely limited or in some circumstances non-existent. The capacity to act as parents in modern society (or at least the ease with which it can be done) is severely limited. It is perfectly true that none of these problems would arise if society was less dependent on written language – in that sense one could 'blame' society rather than the individual – but that is little comfort for those concerned.

The meaning of literacy for those who feel they have not fully acquired it is best expressed in their own words. This is what some young adults told interviewers in a national survey (ALBSU, 1987).

> 'I try to read books but I don't get any difficult words from them. If letters come someone has to read them for me.'

> 'On a motorway I can't read the signs. At work I have problems with filling in the shipping sheets and things.'

'It stops me getting a better job, a more secure one.'

'I'm frightened if someone comes to the door with anything that has to be read. I couldn't fill in an application form for a job if I wanted to.'

For adults who are parents, the difficulties can be particularly distressing.

'My children are starting to read and I can't read stories to them.'

'It's embarrassing – very embarrassing in so many ways. For instance, if I send the kid to a shop I can't write out what I need.'

'I'd like to help my daughter with her school work. I can just cope at the moment but I won't be able to soon.'

The stories of those without literacy tell us what it means for those who do have it. Case studies reported by Peter Johnston (1985) show how much people have to do to compensate for a lack of literacy. At school their coping strategies may include memorising text, listening carefully for oral instructions, bluffing, relying on help from classmates. After leaving school the strategies identified by Johnston were mainly preventative – avoidance of print in any potentially social situation.

> For example, Bill participates in business meetings for which and at which he must read material. His strategy is to be sure to spend some time 'shooting the breeze' with other participants before the meeting to pick up the gist of things. At the meeting he says nothing until asked for his opinion, by which time he has been able to gain enough information to respond. He reported that this also makes him appear conservative and thoughtful. Charlie reads the prices on gas pumps to get the right gas in his car and truck. He cannot read the words but uses the price hierarchy as his information source. Unlike many readers for whom the price is not so relevant, he always remembers the current prices. (Johnston, 1985, p. 159)

Impressive as these strategies are, they do lead to problems. Bill was sometimes found out (trying to read to his young children, reading a paper at work); Charlie sometimes put diesel in his truck by mistake. Both experienced severe anxiety when an encounter with written language could not be avoided.

National Literacy Strategy

So, if it is accepted that there is a literacy problem in terms of the limited competence of a sizeable minority, what is to be done? Action in response to this question – particularly critically aware action – is bound to be of interest to anyone concerned about literacy in education. In the final chapter of this book some ways forward will be considered. Meanwhile the example of one national response will be described. In August 1997 the newly elected Labour government in the UK put forward a 'National Literacy Strategy' for England (Literacy Task Force, 1997b). This can be examined in terms of three things one would expect to be included in any strategy: an analysis of the problem to be tackled, the setting of goals and the identification of means for achieving them.

The Literacy Task Force had earlier offered a limited analysis of the problem in its preliminary report (1997a). It pointed to the 'tail of underachievement' and suggested that the causes were underachieving schools, poor teaching methods, and poor teacher training. It accepted, as a strategic goal, that if a Labour government was elected, and returned for a second term of office, then by the end of that second term (i.e. by 2006), all children leaving primary school should be reaching a reading age of at least 11. This particular formulation of the goal was logically questionable (if there is a spread of reading ability the average cannot, by definition, be exceeded by all members of the age group) but what it appeared to mean was that virtually 100 per cent of 11-year-olds should reach the test level expected at the end of Key Stage 2 of the National Curriculum. The reason for adopting goals and targets for 11-year-olds (rather than, say, 7-year-olds or 14-year-olds) was not explained. The reason given for defining the target in terms of National Curriculum tests was that no one had offered a better alternative.

The specific interim target adopted in the National Literacy Strategy was that 'by 2002, 80% of all 11-year-olds will reach the standards expected of their age in English, (i.e. Level 4) in the Key Stage 2 National Curriculum tests' (Literacy Task Force, 1997b, p. 13). Few would disagree with the Task Force statement that the target is ambitious (assuming of course that the goalposts are not moved). In 1996 the proportion of 11-year-olds reaching Level 4 was 58 per cent. In 1997, 1998 and 1999 it was 63 per cent, 65 per cent and 70 per cent respectively. The trend is clearly in the direction sought but there is, at the time of writing, some way to go.

The means for achieving the target included requiring schools to produce 'literacy action plans', new responsibilities for local education authorities (LEAs), modifying the National Curriculum in other subjects from 2000, more literacy in inital teacher education and teacher professional development, parent involvement (home–school contracts, 20 minutes' daily reading with children, family literacy projects), Summer Literacy Schools, initiatives in secondary schools, and a National Year of Reading, 1998–9.

However, perhaps the two most important means identified in the strategy were the introduction into all primary schools in England of the 'Literacy Hour' and the 'Framework for Teaching'. These two measures had been the main planks of the National Literacy Project introduced by the previous (Conservative) government in 1995 and tried in around 1 per cent of primary schools nationally. The new government's strategy was to extend this to up to 50 per cent of schools and to require every primary school in the country to use the National Literacy Project approach unless they could demonstrate theirs was 'at least as effective'. The Literacy Hour was a daily lesson structured consisting of four parts (10–15 minutes of whole class work with shared text; 10–15 minutes of whole class word or sentence work; 25–30 minutes of group activities; 5–10 minutes of whole class review/sharing/evaluating). The *Framework for Teaching* (DfEE, 1998) specified in considerable detail the programmes of work to be carried out in each term of each primary school year in relation to three levels of work–text, sentence and word. The *Framework* also indicated word lists to be learnt, detailed planning and monitoring procedures.

The introduction of the National Literacy Strategy raises many important issues. There is the appropriateness of the goals and targets set. For such a large scale initiative they seem to have received very little discussion. For example, by setting a criterion for 80 per cent of the population to reach, there is a risk that the remaining 20 per cent will be neglected. Schools performance will be judged by their success with the more able. Yet it is the 20 per cent which appears to be most in need of improved teaching. Raising standards in the general population does not necessarily reduce inequality. There are questions of feasibility which can be answered only through evaluation of the strategy as it is implemented. A very striking feature of the strategy is the degree of central control as the expense of local initiative and the extent of imposition rather than teacher autonomy. The voice of practitioners is not heard much. Evaluation so far appears to be a low priority in comparison with the effort going into implementation. The theoretical justification for the *Framework* was for a long time implicit rather than explicit. Only in 1999 was the relevant research evidence assembled (Beard, 1999).

The 1998 National Literacy Strategy in England brings to the surface in one case all the most fundamental issues in literacy. There is the question of what is worth aiming for in literacy education, what is to count as literacy and how literacy is best taught. It also highlights issues of professional autonomy, parental involvement and evaluation. These are all topics to be addressed in the chapters which follow.

Further Reading

BEARD, R. (1999) *National Literacy Strategy: Review of Research and Other Related Evidence*, London: Department for Education and Employment. Roger Beard of the University of Leeds was commissioned by the National Literacy Strategy to review research studies and inspection reports relevant to its key features. This document is an excellent starting point for considering the evidence base for the Strategy. It clarifies some of the assumptions on which it is based and summarises some of the relevant evidence. In doing so, it makes it possible to appraise those assumptions critically in the light of other evidence and theory.

LITERACY TASK FORCE (1997) *The Implementation of the National Literacy Strategy*, London: Department for Education and Employment. In this key document, the Labour government set out its aims for literacy in education, its specific targets for the duration of its office, and the means whereby it expected to make change. This is a key source for analysing the politics and the policies of literacy in education in England at the turn of the twentieth century.

McClelland, N. and National Literacy Trust (Eds) *Building a Literate Nation: The Strategic Agenda for Literacy Over the Next Five Years*, Stoke-on-Trent: Trentham Books. In 1996, before the UK general election which returned the Labour government which launched so many literacy initiatives, the National Literacy Trust invited various individuals and groups to set out (in the space of 1,200 words) their view of what the national priorities should be in literacy education and how they could be met. This book collects together responses to this challenge. Not all contributors succeeded in looking beyond their own area of special interest to the national picture but enough did to make their contributions interesting when viewed alongside what the new government actually did after taking office in May 1997.

Postman, N. (1970) 'The politics of reading', *Harvard Educational Review*, **40**(2), pp. 244–52. As an antidote to the uncritical assumption that literacy is a 'good' which teachers bestow on their pupils, this article can hardly be bettered. It can be the basis for fruitful discussion if it is read in conjunction with some of the liberatory literature on literacy quoted in this chapter.

Chapter 2

History and Future of Literacy

Overview

It is easy to think of the literacy which is taught in education today as the only kind of literacy there could be. Yet the literacy we see now is only one point in a line of development with a long past and an unknown future. The aim of this chapter is to reflect upon some aspects of the history of literacy and to imagine possibilities for its future. An historical perspective enables us to see taken-for-granted features of written language in a new light. It enables us to examine the claims often heard that literacy brings about economic progress, a higher level of cultural development or political change. Although it is hard to discern how literacy in education may change in the future, it is necessary to be open to the inevitability of there being changes of some kind.

Five Millennia of Written Language

Studying the history of literacy is both important and difficult. It is important because an understanding of how our ancestors created and used writing systems can give us a clearer appreciation of literacy today. It is difficult because it involves trying to puzzle out what happened in the past when many pieces of evidence are missing. It is hard enough to analyse the nature of present day literacy and how it is used in our society. How much harder it is to draw conclusions about ancient societies when all we have are those archaeological fragments which happen to have survived. Yet without an historical perspective it is easy to overlook certain features of present day literacy or fall into the trap of thinking that other features are 'natural' or 'inevitable'.

As far as can be inferred from the archaeological record, the earliest writing systems from which ours evolved can be traced back to around 3300 BC in Mesopotamia and perhaps around the same time in Egypt. There were comparable developments in subsequent millennia in China and in the Americas. Of course, much earlier than 5,000 years ago there were the precursors of writing in cave drawings and carvings and it is an interesting issue to judge at what point such representations can be considered writing. Pictures can tell a story. Also there were mark making systems for counting objects and the passage of time, or identifying possessions. What distinguishes the early writing systems as such is the use of stylised, conventional marks which can be combined in different ways to make different meanings.

The marks in early writing systems were initially pictograms, that is marks with some obvious similarity to whatever they represented but, over time, they became abbreviated or stylised. Others were ideograms, representing ideas or concepts which cannot so easily be pictured. Chinese writing, described as ideographic or logographic, is a present day example of a system where such origins are still visible.

In the earliest writing systems marks represented the world rather in the way that a picture represents an object or a scene. A development of major importance in our system of writing was the use of marks to represent oral language. Like other developments this was probably quite gradual – extending the use of a mark which represented one thing (because it looked like it) to also represent the word for something else (perhaps because the word for the second thing sounded like the word for the first).

From a psychological point of view this development was momentous. It meant that writing became a 'second order symbolic system' in which marks did not represent the world directly but something else – language – which in turn represented the world. Using marks in this way presupposes a certain awareness of language, for example seeing it as consisting of words. It could even be argued that the concept of a 'word' is a result of a culture having a system of writing. Another implication is that anyone learning to read has to grasp the fact that writing is not like pictures. Literacy learners can find this difficult. Vygotsky suggested that learning written language 'must be as much harder than oral speech for the child as algebra is harder than arithmetic' (Vygotsky, 1962, p. 99).

Individual language users have vocabularies of thousands of words, language communities many more. In order to avoid having to learn a specific writing mark for each word, some systems developed marks to represent sounds within words. As words are made up of combinations of a limited number of sounds within a language it is possible to represent words by combinations of marks. This is the principle which underlies alphabetic writing systems such as English. The idea was first developed around 3,000 years ago by the Phoenicians and has reached us via the Greeks and Romans. Alphabetic systems have advantages over logographic systems (e.g. fewer characters to learn) but some disadvantages too (e.g. initial learning may be more difficult).

In human history the development of written language must have meant a change of the same order as the earlier evolution of spoken language. Not only did writing facilitate within-group communication and recording for our ancestors but also it greatly accelerated the process whereby one generation could build upon the accumulated knowledge of previous generations.

There is undoubtedly an association between economic development and literacy. More industrialised societies have a wider spread of literacy in the population. It is sometimes suggested that increases in literacy are actually the cause of economic development but, as Graff (1979, 1987) has shown from historical studies of particular communities, this is too simple a view. Literacy may *follow* economic growth. This should not be surprising since successful economic activity can obviously create a need for record keeping and communication.

Among the earliest surviving examples of writing are agricultural accounts, followed by texts relating to religious and governmental practices (Jean, 1992). The use of written language to express and to explore human experience came later. At first this was in written versions of spoken forms such as stories, myths, songs, poetry or drama – written probably to aid memory. Subsequently, writing became more important in the development of these forms so that the written versions preceded the spoken ones. In many narrative genres (most obviously the novel) the written form stands alone. Children and adults who are able to read such material therefore have access to a vast and intricately depicted range of human experience and reflection stored in the literature of the world. For those who are illiterate in this sense, that door is closed.

The history of literacy is also the history of writing technology. A very wide range of tools (styluses, brushes, pens, typewriters, keyboards) have been used to make marks on a very wide range of surfaces (wood, clay tablets, papyrus, bamboo strips, fabric, stone, parchment, paper, video screens). Technological changes have affected how much can be written, how quickly, and how long the writing lasts. Often what follows is change in the uses for written language, not just more efficient ways of doing the same thing. In Western culture the printing press is celebrated as an invention which transformed literacy by increasing access to written materials but in the history of written language it has to take its place towards the end of a line of other 'inventions' such as clay tablets, ink, paper, quill pens, or book binding. In any case, technological innovation does not act autonomously upon culture. Elisabeth Eisenstein (1982), in a book titled *The Printing Press as an Agent of Change*, makes this point nicely. She rejects a simple cause and effect analysis of how printing changed literacy and society in the fifteenth century and instead shows how it arose from cultural need and how its effects were shaped by culture.

The history of literacy is more than the story of writing systems and technologies. It is also the history of the *uses* to which these have been put. The earliest examples of writing which survive from ancient societies often concern trade, administrative/legal matters and religious uses. More personally expressive uses such as letters, narrative or story are found later.

Literacy and Intellectual History

Some commentators have argued that literacy enables societies to reach a higher level of intellectual achievement. In one sense this is obviously true for it is hard to see how scientific and cultural thinking could get very far at all unless each generation is able to build upon the discoveries of previous ones. But some claims have gone further than this. Much has been made of the distinction between 'oral societies' and 'literate societies'. One eighteenth-century historian wrote, 'The use of letters is the principal circumstance that distinguishes a civilized people from a herd of savages, incapable of knowledge or reflection' (Gibbon, 1776/1896, p. 218). Subsequent writers have made the same point more gently.

> The civilization created by the Greeks and Romans was the first on the earth's surface which was founded upon the activity of the common reader; the first to be equipped with the means of adequate expression in the inscribed word; the first to be able to place the inscribed word in general circulation; the first, in short, to become literate in the full meaning of that term, and to transmit its literacy to us. (Havelock, 1982, p. 40)

The claim here is that there is a great divide between literate and other societies. David Barton (1994), in his book *Literacy: An Introduction to the Ecology of Written Language*, sets it out as follows.

> An important aspect of the great divide proposal is the notion that modern literate societies are fundamentally different in many aspects of social organisation from earlier, simpler societies, and that these differences are ultimately attributable to literacy. Aspects of modern societies that are said to hinge upon the existence of literacy include the development of democracy, certain forms of political organization and the possibility for technological advance. (Barton, 1994, p. 117)

Barton goes on to criticise this claim as grossly oversimplified and lacking in evidence. For example, one version, which he terms the 'Greek' argument, makes much of the simultaneous emergence in Greece of an alphabetic writing system, new forms of logic and forms of democracy. Yet historical research has established that the first two developed much earlier than the third, both in Greece and in other societies.

A more sophisticated view of the intellectual consequences of literacy in society has been put forward by David Olson (1994). He argues that literacy has had profound intellectual consequences but his argument rests on a point made earlier in this chapter, that writing is a way of representing language. Hence being literate means having a certain sort of awareness of language (e.g. that it consists of words, sounds). Writing has proved to be a very effective way of representing what people say but one of its weaknesses is that it is hard to capture in writing *how* people say things. Olson gives the example of the statement, 'Dinner is at eight'. Our writing system is perfectly adequate for indicating what was said but it is poor at indicating whether the words should be taken as a prediction, a statement, an invitation, or a promise. Yet in real life if we heard someone say, 'Dinner is at eight', we would probably have no difficulty in using non-verbal cues to tell which of these possibilities was meant. Something gets left out in the writing (something which philosophers term the 'illocutionary force' of a speech act). Olson suggests, that in order to overcome this weakness, users of written language were forced to create a vocabulary and conceptual system to describe how people meant words to be taken – their mental states/feelings/intentions and so on – and that this created an enhanced awareness of individual psychology.

> The history of literacy, in other words, is the struggle to recover what was lost in simple transcription. The solution is to turn non-lexical properties of speech

such as stress and intonation into lexical ones; one announces that the proposition expressed is to be taken as an assumption or an inference and whether it is to be taken metaphorically or literally. But in making those structures explicit, that is representing them as concepts, and marking them in a public language, those structures themselves become objects of reflection. (Olson, 1994, p. 111)

In his book, *The World on Paper*, Olson (1994) speculates further about how literacy changed awareness of language as a tool of scientific enquiry in the seventeenth and eighteenth centuries, thereby paving the way for the achievements of modern science. The issues are complex but Olson offers an intriguing and stimulating argument that is likely to fuel debates in this field for some time to come. He concludes his book thus,

there seems little doubt that writing and reading played a critical role in producing the shift from thinking about things to thinking about representations of those things, that is, thinking about thought. Our modern conception of the world and our modern conception of ourselves are, we may say, by-products of the invention of a world on paper. (Olson, 1994, p. 282)

The Spread of Literacy within Societies

For most of its history written language has been the preserve of the powerful in society and the way in which it has been used has reflected their interests. Only in modern times have the least powerful been expected to acquire literacy and even then the kind of literacy thought appropriate for them may differ from that exercised by the powerful.

In nineteenth-century Britain for example, working class political aspirations included a concern with literacy as a part of universal education and universal suffrage. One of the leading Chartists, William Lovett, in 1841 made detailed proposals for a method of teaching reading and writing. It was intended to replace learning 'by rote, without understanding' with a 'closer connection of words and things', with meaningful learning. Crucially, however, this was coupled with a political vision of education for the working classes which went beyond 'the mere teaching of "reading, writing, and arithmetic"' and which sought to remove 'the obstacles to their liberty and impediments to their happiness which ignorance still presents'. Lovett wanted to develop literacy because he believed it would enable the oppressed to understand what was being done to them.

The fact of an insignificant portion of the people arrogating to themselves the political rights and powers of the whole, and persisting in making and enforcing such laws as are favourable to their own 'order', and inimical to the interests of the many, affords a strong argument in proof of the ignorance of those who submit to such injustice. (Lovett, 1841, quoted in Simon, 1972, p. 245)

The problematic, even contentious, nature of current school literacy is often hidden and it is hard to imagine alternative conceptions of it. However, one way to appreciate the *constructed* nature of school literacy is to take an historical perspective. In the past, there certainly were different conceptions of school literacy. An interesting issue has been the teaching of writing – particularly for working class children. For example, in the 1790s, Hannah More, an influential figure in the establishment of Sunday schools for working class children, is quoted by Brian Simon as insisting that they should not be taught to write at all. 'I allow of no writing for the poor. My object is not to make them fanatics, but to train up the lower classes in habits of industry and piety' (quoted in Simon, 1960, p. 133).

Simon also quotes Andrew Bell, who became superintendent of the 'National Society' which promoted church schools for the poor. In 1805 Bell argued that children should be taught to read (the Bible) but he felt differently about writing. 'It is not proposed that the children of the poor be educated in an expensive manner, or even taught to write and to cypher' (quoted in Simon, 1960, p. 133).

Later in the century, the state became involved in funding mass education for the working classes. In 1862 this led to the notorious 'Revised Code' which stipulated what level of attainment was required of children for a school to be funded. There were six levels or 'standards'. From a twenty-first century perspective these were not very ambitious but one striking feature from a late twentieth century perspective is the fact that reading was seen as *oral reading*. Also, writing was conceived of as *writing from dictation*. The idea of pupils writing something of their own does not appear to have been valued. In fact it was many years before 'composition' was considered appropriate in the elementary school curriculum, and then at first only for older pupils (Birchenough, 1914).

Now, several generations on, there is again a national curriculum in England. It seems obvious that the current version is not as restrictive as the last one at the end of the nineteenth century. But who can say how it will be regarded from a vantage point at the end of the twenty-first century? Even now a struggle is taking place between those who wish children taught phonic skills more explicitly and at an earlier age and those who would rather emphasise meaning and engagement in the early school years; between those who want older children to learn to appreciate certain texts in a national 'literary heritage' and those who prefer a wider choice. The only certain things about any changes which are made is that they will be decided politically and that they will not be permanent. The point is that what counts as school literacy at any particular time is not a given but the result of social processes.

The Future of Literacy

Now to something which does not exist – at least something which does not exist yet – literacy in the future. We are living in a period when literacy is changing particularly rapidly and no one can be certain what will happen next. This part of the book therefore depends more than the rest on the interests, prejudices and particular limitations of the author. The aim is to share some reflections about current trends and some speculations about the future in order to increase awareness that literacy really is changing in front of our eyes, and to pose the question, 'Where is it leading?'

We can begin by reflecting on changes which have occurred in the recent past – in our own lifetimes – and then confront the question, 'Is this the end of literacy?' The end may not be nigh but profound changes are underway in reading, in writing and in the uses of written language.

Changes in our Lifetimes

There is a temptation for every generation to believe that its particular historical period is momentous in one way or another but there are strong reasons for believing that the period of the second half of the twentieth century and the dawn of the twenty-first has been, and will continue to be, truly dramatic for literacy. Think back to the time when you first learned to read and write. Compare the literacy technology and resources available to you then to what you use now, and to what is available for literacy learners today. Think what has changed.

In my case I have been struck by the extent of technological changes. I started school in England in the 1950s when writing involved steel nib pens, inkwells and blotting paper. A time traveller from the sixteenth century, familiar with quill pens and the then-new material of paper, would have been entirely comfortable with this technology for mark making. True, pencils were used in reception and infant classes but by older pupils only for 'rough' work. Ball-point pens were still expensive and frowned upon in school on the grounds that they encouraged sloppy handwriting. Only a few children acquired fountain pens from home before the end of primary school. Consequently, the activity of writing for children was often laborious and the results could be unsightly. Contrast that with the experience of children today who have much more convenient writing implements – including not just ball-point pens but fibre-tipped ones too, in many colours – and plentiful supplies of different kinds of paper. Fountain pens have come and gone and are now novelty items. Even more dramatic, some children's earliest writing experiences today are with computers, using keyboards and making marks on screen with all the power of word processing software for amending text and printing out perfect hard copy. Today, even the smallest schools in Britain have computers, printers and photocopiers whereas in the 1950s, at best, they had manual typewriters and duplicating machines.

In reading too there has been an enormous change. In the 1950s the amount of material for young readers in classrooms was very limited and I cannot remember anyone being excited by the content. Today, advances in printing technology have meant that there are many more books for children and they are better written, illustrated and produced than ever before. The revolution in children's publishing in the 1970s and 1980s meant new markets, the emergence of new authors committed to engaging young readers, and new genres integrating text with colour illustrations and graphics. This revealed the poverty of traditional reading schemes and prompted many teachers of young children to rethink their entire approach to teaching reading by basing it more on so-called 'real books'. There have also been changes in children's out of school reading which, for many families, may be more dramatic than those affecting in-school reading. Some families are able to buy the new books for children but even in poorer families children are now growing up in a world saturated with environmental print on advertisements, notices, packaging, junk mail and television.

Even in recent years as an adult, I have experienced rapid change in the technology of literacy. Most of what I now write and read has been produced, processed, stored or transmitted by methods such as photocopying, word processing, laser printing, fax, computer networks or electronic mail – methods which have become routine in my workplace since the late 1980s. Carbon paper, duplicating machines, card indexes and telegrams have slipped into history. Manual typewriters are at the point of extinction even for domestic use. Staff and students in higher education have to keep up with almost monthly developments in information technology (e.g. in libraries, computer networks, CD-ROM, the internet) which affect both teaching and research.

Does Literacy Have a Future?

It is sometimes suggested that reading and writing will not be very important in the future, particularly as the full impact of information technology is felt. It is certainly true that there are certain contexts in which many of us now have less use for written language than did our parents' generation (or perhaps even than we did ourselves in the 1970s). For example, one can think of the way in which the increased use of the telephone (and the availability of mobile phones, message and voice-mail facilities) has meant a decline in the writing of all kinds of letters or the way in which television and video viewing has replaced the reading of books. Yet we have to be careful about concluding that this means less writing and reading. The telephone has also led to the fax machine which reinstates written language. Television has also provided new reasons for reading (e.g. programme listings), new genres (mini-reviews of films, print in advertisements), new ways of reading (teletext), and has stimulated new appetites for books (e.g. classic novels, cookery books). It is safer to conclude that literacy use is *different* rather than less than it was formerly.

Computer based information technology will continue to change the uses and necessity for written language but, again, it is likely that it will decrease some uses while at the same time stimulating others. For example, written language has recently taken on a new importance as a method of human–machine communication – usually in inputting instructions or data through a computer keyboard (i.e. writing) and in reading from a screen. This may eventually be superseded by other methods based on graphic displays and direct voice input/output but for reasons of speed and efficiency these will almost certainly still require literacy at least in being able to read messages on screen. The idea that advances in information technology reduce the need for literacy ignores the fact that a great deal of this technology is devoted to the storage, organisation, and processing of text. On-line help systems are often heavily text dependent. Also, information technology appears to generate a huge amount of ancillary printed material in the form of user manuals, specialist magazines and other documentation.

David Reinking (1994) has suggested that there are four fundamental differences between printed and electronic texts. First, he points out that while it has often been suggested that readers interact with text in a metaphorical sense, in the case of electronic text this can be literally true, for example in the way readers can respond to some text by switching to other texts via 'hot links'. Second, it is possible for electronic texts to guide or restrict the reading path according to educational or other criteria, e.g. requiring re-reading of passages if comprehension questions are not answered correctly. Third, the structure of electronic text can be radically different in 'hypertext' (to be discussed in a later section). Fourth, electronic texts often employ new symbolic elements – not just illustrations but video clips and other graphics, including text 'navigation' aids. One can argue about whether or not these features of electronic literacy are desirable but that they have arrived and that they represent a radical shift seems beyond argument.

Advances in the technology of visual media – films, videos – may at first sight appear to diminish the importance of conventional literacy but, as Colin MacCabe (1998) has argued, this is to ignore the complex interplay between writing and visual media – in both production and reception.

> The interdependence between print and image is much more than a simple reliance on books as source material for films. At every stage of film-making, the written work is central to the production process. Our culture encourages this promiscuity of media, and the computer mixes image and print in ever more complex ways. (MacCabe, 1998, p. 14)

In her study of differences in the literacy of boys and girls, Elaine Millard (1997) tells how she came to rethink both the nature of literacy and the connection between print literacy and electronic literacy.

> Literacy was a process that I associated only with immersion in books. As the enquiry progressed I changed my opinion of the computer's distracting influence, and even modified my view of the role of computer games, as negative competitors with literacy activities. This was because I found that working with personal computers not only often involved on-screen reading activities, but that it also engaged young players in a secondary reading of complex texts in order to update their hardware or to progress onto higher levels of difficult games. (Millard, 1997, p. 153)

The nature of literacy in a culture is repeatedly redefined as the result of technological changes. Throughout history the introduction of new materials (stone tablets, skins, papyrus, paper) and new mark making methods (scratching, chiselling, ink, the printing press, typewriters, ball-points, laser printers, and so on) has meant both new users and new uses for written language. The consequences of such changes can be very complex – not just in terms of more literacy but different literacy (Eisenstein, 1982). Technology begins by making it easier to do familiar things; then it creates opportunities to do new things. Our literacy today is consequently very different from that of medieval England not just because the printing press is more efficient than having scribes copy manuscripts in monasteries but also because printing and other technologies have stimulated entirely new uses for written language (e.g. tax forms, novels, postcards, advertisements) unimagined by medieval society. If the past is any guide to the future, we should expect information technology to transform literacy rather than eradicate it. To get some idea of the transformations which may be on the way, let us consider in turn the futures of writing and reading.

The Future of Writing

There are two main changes to consider in writing. The first concerns how text is produced and processed; the second, how it is transmitted to others. Both may have far reaching consequences.

Regarding the first change, I am writing this chapter on a standard 1990s word processing package which allows me to do things which a few years ago would have been regarded as quite magical but which are now taken for granted. I can write as fast as I can type. I can delete text and it vanishes – completely – leaving no trace. I can insert extra text anywhere and the computer moves other text to accommodate it. I can move text from one point in a document to another. A spelling check can eliminate many of my mistakes. I have an enormous choice of page layouts, print fonts and sizes, paragraph and line formats. The screen display is graphical (showing text proportionally spaced and characters in different fonts). It is easy to insert other graphics. There are endless possibilities for editing and polishing. It is almost easier to tinker with the text than leave it alone. When I have done as much as I wish, a touch of a virtual button produces a printed paper copy (or multiple copies if I wish) of a quality which only professional print shops could produce a few years ago.

I see this page on screen virtually as readers see it now in its printed paper version (as wysiwyg – 'what you see is what you get'). However, unlike all previous mark making systems in the history of writing I am not really making marks on anything at all. Until it is printed out, this text exists only in electronic form.

> The bits of text are simply not on a human scale. Electronic technology removes or abstracts the writer and reader from the text. If you hold a magnetic or optical disc up to the light, you will not see text at all . . . In the electronic medium several layers of sophisticated technology must intervene between the writer or reader and the coded text. There are so many levels of deferral that the reader or writer is hard put to identify the text at all: is it on the screen, in the transistor memory, or on disk? (Bolter, 1990, pp. 42–3)

The technology is powerful because software plus computer and video screen make it look as if the writing is onto paper but all that exists is virtual writing. The capacity of information technology to mimic conventional forms of communication can be taken further in virtual books or (as in some university courses these days) 'virtual seminars'.

The implications of this power for writing in the future include the following.

Word processing obviously makes it easier to revise and edit writing. For those who wish to write better – whether they are striving to be more effective, more economical, more persuasive, or whatever – the possibility of being able to try a version of a text and to amend it without significant physical labour is obviously going to make it easier to accomplish their goals. Optimists will see word processing as, on the whole, likely to lead to more writers and to better writing in the future but it can also make life easier for those who write carelessly.

Being able to create and insert non-text graphics in a document could have far-reaching consequences. We have grown up with a very text-bound concept of writing because the production of graphics (illustrations, diagrams, embellishments) has hitherto been so difficult for ordinary writers. Yet graphics has become very important – even dominant – in newspapers, magazines, advertisements, packaging, notices and so on. Perhaps everyone will be 'writing' with images in this way in the future and the nature of writing itself will change.

The fact that it is easier to print superb quality documents using standard word processing packages (never mind desktop publishing systems) means a certain democratisation of literacy. Anyone can be a publisher – well, almost a publisher (mass production and distribution still matter) – and to that extent the authority of the printed text is no longer the preserve of the few.

Thus far it has been assumed that writing in the future involves getting text on to paper but of course that is now a limited conception of writing. The second major change in writing is how it is transmitted. If writing is encoded electronically it can be transmitted that way from one output device (terminal, computer, screen, printer) to another.

This morning, working at my desk in the university, I replied to messages from three work colleagues using email (electronic mail). One of them works in the same building as me but the other two work in universities in the United States and South Africa. The procedure was identical in each case. I read their message on my computer screen, clicked on an icon to reply, typed my reply and then clicked on another icon to send the message. My colleague at Sheffield would have been able to read my reply within seconds; it would probably not take much longer for the overseas messages to reach their destinations too. Not only is this kind of 'letter' astonishingly quick, but also it is entirely paperless. No time is spent hunting for notepaper, writing the message, making a copy, folding it, placing it in an envelope, stamping it, and remembering to post it. Eliminating these stages not only speeds up the process of writing letters but also, like earlier technological developments in literacy, changes the uses for written language. It encourages a casual, immediate style of communication and it becomes possible, for example, to sustain a research collaboration with people thousands of miles away.

The use of email is part of wider set of possibilities for reading, writing and communicating via interrelated networks of computers across the world which is the internet. It means that those with access to the technology can search distant databases and 'bulletin boards' serving specialist interests. Already, more than 100 million people worldwide use the internet to read documents, journal articles or books which will never be published in paper form and many of them publish to the world through their websites.

The Future of Reading

In reading the main change to be considered is in the nature of text itself. We have grown up with some taken-for-granted assumptions about text which now need to be changed.

It is perfectly possible to read a document – this book, for example – on a computer much as one would read it on paper. The screen image can look quite like the printed version, pressing the PageUp and PageDown keys is akin to turning real pages, and one can 'turn' to specified page numbers. However, the computer permits other reading possibilities. Some of the simplest, available within most current word processing software, are jumping to points in the text where a specific word or phrase is used or viewing two widely separated sections of a document simultaneously, in adjacent 'windows'. There are no exact parallels to these strategies in reading printed text. More advanced software, now routinely available, allows one to go further. For example, the readers can point to certain words or symbols (with a cursor or 'mouse') and immediately gain access to another text. This is useful if they wish to consult a footnote or read another document which has been cited. It might be possible to repeat the procedure with the second text to access a third, and so on. Imagine being able to do this with all the readings and references for a university course. As readers progress through a document in the order which suit them best, with digressions into other documents, they are in effect creating their own version of the document. The technology can allow them to save their particular pathway for future reference with any notes they may wish to add (without affecting the original versions which remain available too).

It no longer seems adequate to refer to what is being read as 'text' in the conventional sense. Instead the term hypertext (as opposed to print text) has gained currency. Tuman (1992) also distinguishes between what he calls print literacy and on-line literacy to distinguish the ways of reading and writing associated with print and computer-based uses of written language.

In hypertext readers' pathways through a text need not be linear – they can take sections in whatever order they choose and integrate several different texts. There may be no order other than the ones created by the readers.

The linearity of print text can certainly be a problem for writers struggling to work out the best order in which to set out interconnected ideas and trying to avoid referring to ideas which have not already been introduced to the reader or wanting to define several terms simultaneously. It is a considerable challenge to linearise a set of concepts which are interlinked as a structure in thinking. A 70,000 word book is essentially a thin string of typing up to a mile in length – the fact that it is arranged in 6-inch segments (i.e. lines), 30 or so to a page, disguises this linear quality. A good writer can make it easy for readers to follow the string, picking up needed information and ideas in the easiest possible order. Also, if the writer provides 'signposts' (a preface, a list of contents, chapter headings, sub-headings, clear paragraph structure, and so on) readers do not have to follow the string closely but can skip bits and revisit earlier segments if they wish. However, writers of print texts cannot usually rely on such jumping back and forth to make the text readable – they have to provide at least one clear, 'recommended' route through the text.

One may ask, 'Does hypertext eliminate the need for linearity in writing?' Some enthusiasts would answer, 'yes' and see it as a virtue of hypertext that it frees the reader from the control of the writer because there is no single reading or mean-ing of a text. One example, quoted by Tuman (1992, p. 55), is Nelson (1987) who argues the case thus:

> Imagine a new libertarian literature with alternative explanations so anyone can choose the pathway or approach that bests suits him or her; with ideas accessi-ble and interesting to everyone, so that a new richness and freedom can come to the human experience; imagine a rebirth of literacy. (Nelson, 1987, p. 1/4)

One could take the contrary view, however. Even in hypertext some processes must operate to select certain texts and not others; to facilitate certain paths and not others. Also, the absence of linearity might be a loss as well as a gain. With-out the discipline of linearity, writers may not be forced to develop clear concepts or to iron out contradictions within their arguments. Readers may consequently find it more difficult, not less, to grasp the writer's meaning. This could be par-ticularly problematic in teaching situations.

Implications for Understanding Literacy Today

Many of the future possibilities discussed in this chapter are either in an early stage of development or confined to relatively privileged groups. For example, in education developments have gone further in universities than in adult basic edu-cation or primary schools; many people have access to personal computers but not all have CD-ROM facilities and internet connections. Change may be on the way but until it arrives is there any point in bothering about it? There is – for the following reasons.

All our literacy students will end up using written language tomorrow in ways very different from those we can teach them today. This applies to adult students – even older ones who may, for example, be taught to write using conventional pen and paper technology but who may go on to use internet facilities at a local library. It applies much more strongly to younger students and children who, if development proceeds in the next fifty years as it has in the past fifty, will use written language in ways which we cannot even imagine. What matters in this context is that we teach what is important about written language – those essentials which can be expected to endure in future contexts. These could include the ideas that the value of written language depends on what we want to do with it, that all texts can be read critically, that there are many genres, that literacy has a potential for liberation, that writing can aid thinking, that reading can be enjoyable, that public writing is for readers not writers, and so on.

Almost all pronouncements about literacy – its nature, use, development, and how it should be taught – have now to be considered as provisional and temporary. Whatever we think or say about literacy is bound to be a reflection of our particular historical period with its technology and uses for written language. To see how this might be so consider how someone in the sixteenth century might have seen the arrival of printed books. Marshall McLuhan (1962) speculated that the reaction could have been as follows.

> Could a portable, private instrument like the new book take the place of the book one made by hand and memorized as one made it? Could a book which could be read quickly and even silently take the place of book read slowly aloud? Could students trained by such printed books measure up to the skilled orators and disputants produced by manuscript means? (McLuhan, 1962, p. 145)

The point is that our own view of literacy today could be just as much shaped by our conceptions of the uses we have for written language.

A major research task is to elucidate the real nature of the changes which we are now encountering and which are likely to get more pronounced in the twenty-first century. What, in fact, are the new demands for using written language in the workplace or the school? How will it affect processes of learning and teaching? What are the political implications?

How is information technology exacerbating or reducing social inequalities in literacy? In the 1980s, Hannon and Wooler expressed these concerns.

> There is every reason to believe that the gulf between children of different social classes will widen. Access to IT devices in school could be reasonably equal for all children (although our experience of the distribution of other educational resources may give grounds for doubt) but there are bound to be huge differences in home use of computers and computer-based equipment like video disks and database terminals. Entire 'curricula' are likely to be marketed by software houses or large publishing corporations. The result will be fatal to the opportunities of many working class children who will be disadvantaged in terms of the sheer amount of time they will be able to spend learning via computers. Economic differences between families are likely to be translated even more directly into educational differences. (Hannon and Wooler, 1985, p. 93)

Much of this had indeed come to pass. What these authors did not foresee, however, was expansion of the internet which – arguably – has some potential for equalising access to electronically stored knowledge if families can pass the threshold of computer internet connection. Even then, it must be admitted that differences in terms of computer skills, adult support and cultural know-how may be too great for some children ever to overcome.

Landow (1992) points out that 'almost all authors on hypertext who touch upon the political implications of hypertext assume that the technology is essentially democratizing and that it therefore supports some sort of decentralized, liberated existence' (Landow, 1992, p. 33). On the other hand, Michael Apple (1986) has suggested that

> computers involve ways of thinking that are primarily technical. The more the new technology transforms the classroom in its own image, the more a technical logic will replace critical political and ethical understanding. (Apple, 1986, p. 171)

Those involved in teaching literacy – in any capacity – need to think about how they are preparing learners for literacy in the future. What assumptions are made about the future? Are there specific aspects of literacy which deserve more emphasis? How would it be possible to provide this?

Determining the actual, as opposed to the possible, impact of the new technology on literacy could be one of the most interesting research challenges in this field in the twenty-first century.

Further Reading

BARTON, D. (1994) *Literacy: An Introduction to the Ecology of Written Language*, Oxford: Blackwell. This book takes a broadly interdisciplinary view of literacy. It therefore includes some account of the history of reading and writing, stressing the social rather than the technical, aspects of literacy. It is valuable for its treatment of the issues in this chapter and also in other chapters.

BROOKFIELD, K. (1993) *Writing*, London: Dorling Kindersley/British Library. This and G. Jean's book (see below) are histories of writing from earliest times to the present. They are not themselves scholarly works but they include references to other sources and they are immediately accessible – and ideal for browsing – on account of the very high quality of colour illustrations.

EISENSTEIN, E.L. (1982) *The Printing Press as an Agent of Change: Communications and Cultural Transformations in Early-Modern Europe*, Cambridge: Cambridge University Press. This is a major study which shows the complex interplay between technology and culture in a celebrated episode in the history of literacy. Many of the issues apply to other historical innovations in literacy.

JEAN, G. (1992) *Writing: The Story of Alphabets and Scripts* (see K. Brookfield's reference above), London: Thames and Hudson.

MANGUEL, A. (1996) *A History of Reading,* London: Flamingo. Although this book covers literacy from earliest times to the present, it is not a history in a conventional sense of being a chronological narrative. Instead there are some twenty chapters, each being wide ranging essays reflecting on various literacy topics, emphasising in particular the social uses of literacy and individuals' experience of reading and writing. It is a compilation and synthesis of interesting pieces of information and insights.

REINKING, D. et al. (Eds) (1998) *Handbook of Literacy and Technology: Transformations in the Post-Typographic World*, London: Lawrence Erlbaum Associates. This book seeks to explore how electronic forms of reading and writing my be transforming literacy, as the world moves into a new century in which printed texts may no longer be dominant.

TOPPING, K. (1997) 'Electronic literacy in school and home: A look into the future', *Reading Online*.
http: //www.readingonline.org/international/future/index.html Reading Online is an electronic journal published by the International Reading Association. This article in the journal is a hypertext introduction to some of the issues to be considered in the move from print literacy to electronic literacy with particular reference to family literacy and home–school links in the future.

Chapter 3

One Literacy or Many?

Overview

Underlying the common view of literacy there tends to be an assumption that it is something which is unvarying and unitary but this is challenged by an alternative, pluralist view of literacy. Both the unitary and pluralist views provide undoubted insights as well as raising conceptual difficulties. Can they be reconciled? In this chapter it is suggested that they stem from two different conceptions – of literacy as a skill and of literacy as a social practice. Each conception is valid but neither on its own is sufficient for understanding literacy in education. Implications for thinking about the literacy curriculum are considered.

The Unitary View of Literacy

Consider the following half-dozen quotations, taken from books about literacy. They are by authors with very different perspectives, and writing about different aspects of literacy, yet they all confidently refer to a single thing, 'literacy', which they assume readers will be able to recognise.

> By the learning of literacy, we mean the development of spoken language and written language from their origins in early infancy to their mastery as systems of representation for communication with others. (Garton and Pratt, 1998, p. 1)

> In the past 20 years, researchers and scholars working in early literacy have constructed a powerful knowledge base, concluding that children come to know literacy through their daily and mundane experiences in their particular social, cultural, religious, economic, linguistic, and literate societies. (Goodman, 1990, p. 115)

> To assess literacy properly, you need an objective definition of literacy for each age tested, up to and including adults. This means setting an absolute standard of literacy which is independent of the population's reading level, unlike standardized tests which simply reflect a population's ability. (McGuinness, 1998, p. 8)

> The success of a literacy campaign can only be fully evaluated in terms of its sustained impact. Too often people who pick up basic skills in well-publicized campaigns, lose those skills through disuse in the silent aftermath. Either no follow-up is available for consolidation, or the skills learnt find no applications.

In rural areas, people who have spent their lives without the written word find little value in the techniques of reading and writing unless other aspects of their lives change. But if literacy is sustained it can provide the tools for people to make these changes themselves. (Archer and Costello, 1990, p. 33)

The challenge in teaching literacy is to consider widely and appropriately a variety of perspectives, to provide the kind of balanced judgements which will best help the children in our care. (Beard, 1993, p. 3)

Children create their literacy in contexts where: literacy is a meaningful event for them; where they see people participating in literacy for real purposes and with enjoyment; where people are prepared to discuss their literacy activities; where there are opportunities for children to participate in literacy; where child-initiated literacy behaviour is welcomed by adults; and where children's literate efforts are treated seriously. (Hall, 1987, p. 73)

Not only do these extracts unproblematically refer to 'literacy' as if everyone knows what it is but also they take it for granted that there is an 'it' which can be referred to. The 'it' is sometimes taken to be a skill or competence – the ability to use written language. According to this view the actual uses which particular readers and writers have for that competence is something which can be separated from the competence itself. It may be acknowledged that the uses depend on a complex of social, economic and political factors affecting the particular user of written language but it is suggested that the competence is intrinsically neutral.

The Pluralist View of Literacy

Despite its common sense appeal the unitary view of literacy presents some problems. The previous chapter showed that when literacy is viewed from an historical perspective, and when possibilities in the future are also contemplated, its nature is not so fixed. There are variations in the technology for mark making, in the conventions developed within different writing systems and in the uses for written language. If these can vary from one time to another, and also perhaps from one place to another, might the differences between variants be so great that what we are faced with is *different literacies* rather than different versions of a single thing called literacy?

One reason for taking this view is based on the fact that literacy is embedded in culture and since there are many cultures it could be argued that there are many literacies. This is not just a matter of variation in the particular written language or script being used or variation in subject matter. Of more significance can be variation in the *uses* of that written language. Even within countries such as Britain, the United States or Australia, and even among those inhabitants for whom English is a first language, there are different cultures and sub-cultures. They can be distinguished, for example, in terms of region, ethnicity, occupation, social class, gender and possibly social or institutional context. In each case the potential uses for written language may be the same but the pattern of actual uses may differ markedly. Writing for publication (in books or newspapers) is more common in middle class than in working class culture. Writing of personal letters may not vary so much. Reading of novels may well vary, but reading for information may not.

Two studies, among many, can illustrate how literacy is shaped by culture. In a classic study in the United States, Shirley Brice Heath (1983) has shown that *what* children learn at home about literacy can vary enormously according to the culture and values of their communities. She carried out a lengthy ethnographic study in the southern United States of two small neighbouring communities ('Trackton', black working class; 'Roadville', white working class) and found that their uses for literacy differed significantly from each other (and also from that of the 'mainstream' town community). For example, in 'Trackton', children were more likely to be involved in literacy events with several participants; in 'Roadville' bedtime stories were more common. Heath showed how these differences were rooted deep in culture and in patterns of oral language use. Despite having preschool literacy experiences, children from the two working class communities had difficulties with school literacy because their home literacies were not as congruent with the school literacy as was the case for the 'mainstream' community. The importance of this study goes far beyond what it tells us about literacy in the 1970s in two particular communities (which may no longer exist). It shows that children anywhere can learn about literacy before school, and out of school, but their literacy learning need not be the same. In a British study of older children Elaine Millard (1997) has shown how boys' and girls' uses of written language differ in terms of their choice of reading, their leisure activities and their preference for alternative forms of 'narrative distraction' such as television programmes, video recordings and computer games. The boys in Millard's study read fewer books and their preferred genres were not as congruent with school literacy (at least in terms of the English curriculum) as that of girls but in the long run Millard suggests that boys may be staking a claim to the more powerful, electronic forms of communication of the future. Although Millard does talk of boys and girls being 'differently literate', neither she nor Heath talk of different 'literacies'. Other writers, however, do discuss the issues in these terms.

Among theorists who contend that it is seriously misleading to use the word literacy when there are marked differences in what it means for different users in different contexts is Colin Lankshear (1987). He has challenged the unitary view as follows.

> There is no single, unitary referent for 'literacy'. Literacy is not the name for a finite technology, set of skills, or any other 'thing'. We should recognise, rather, that there are many specific literacies, each comprising an identifiable set of socially constructed practices based upon print and organised around beliefs about how the skills of reading and writing may or, perhaps, should be used. (Lankshear, 1987, p. 58)

David Barton (1994) has argued for a focus on what he terms 'literacy practices' – common social practices associated with written language in a culture – and from this has argued for a pluralist view.

> Where these different practices cluster into coherent groups it is very useful to talk in terms of them as being *different literacies*. A literacy is a stable, coherent, identifiable configuration of practices such as *legal literacy*, or the literacy of specific workplaces. (Barton, 1994, p. 38, original italics)

James Gee (1996) argues that being able to read or write always means being able to read or write *something*, and, furthermore, if one examines specific instances, one finds that the way something is read or written always depends upon the reader's previous cultural experience of such texts.

> There are obviously many abilities here, each of them a type of literacy, one of a set of literacies. (Gee, 1996, p. 41)

Denny Taylor (1997) has put the case for recognising different literacies in the context of families' uses for written language.

> Descriptive studies of families and literacy in many different countries with many different cultural traditions have changed narrow preconceptions. These studies show that each family is an original, that there is a seemingly infinite variety of patterns of cooperation and domestic organization, and that flexible household arrangements are often an adaptive response to an uncertain world. Within family settings there are both multiple literacies and multiple literacy practices. (Taylor, 1997, p. 1)

David Barton and Mary Hamilton (1998) made use of the idea of different literacies in their detailed ethnographic study of literacy practices in one town in England.

> Looking at different literacy events it is clear that literacy is not the same in all contexts; rather, there are different literacies . . . within a given culture, there are different literacies associated with different domains of life. Contemporary life can be analysed in a simple way into domains of activity, such as home, school, work-place. (Barton and Hamilton, 1998, p. 9)

One consequence of 'seeing' different literacies is that it focuses attention on ways in which 'school literacy' may differ from, and may even be in conflict with, 'home literacy', 'community literacy' or 'workplace literacy'. For some families – specifically middle class ones – there may be a high degree of congruence between home literacy, school literacy and workplace literacy but for other families school literacy may be far removed from that which they encounter at home or at work. This makes problematic the issue of whether some literacies can be regarded as more valuable than others (where literacy is viewed as unitary this issue tends to be hidden). In particular it forces a rethinking of the importance to be given to 'school literacy'.

Taylor (1997) suggests that what is sometimes seen as people's lack of literacy is actually them having the 'wrong' literacy, i.e. a literacy different from the dominant ones.

> Some of these literacies have become powerful and dominant, while others have been constrained and devalued. The problem is not so much a lack of literacy, but a lack of social justice. Local knowledge is not always appreciated and local literacies are not always recognized. (Taylor, 1997, p. 4)

Street (1984) has distinguished what he terms 'autonomous' and 'ideological' models of literacy. The 'autonomous' model embodies assumptions often made by educators and psychologists (that literacy alone provides certain cognitive benefits, that its development is unidirectional, that it is separable from schooling, and that it brings about economic, social and political progress). Street argues that this model over-generalises from one narrow, culture-specific literacy practice.

Also associated with the pluralist view is rejection of the idea of literacy as a neutral skill. Lankshear (1987) has criticised the idea in these terms:

> I argue that literacy is the uses to which it is put and the conceptions which shape and reflect its actual use. Once this is admitted we do more than merely achieve relief from the gross reification of literacy involved in the literacy-as-a-neutral-skill-or-technology view. In addition, we are freed to ask a whole range of questions that we are effectively discouraged from asking if we assume that literacy is neutral. For we can now entertain the possibility that the forms reading and writing take in daily life are related to the wider operation of power and patterns of interest within society. (Lankshear, 1987, p. 50)

Gee (1996) has argued in a similar vein:

> the traditional view of literacy as the ability to read and write rips literacy out of its sociocultural contexts and treats it as an asocial cognitive skill with little or nothing to do with human relationships. It cloaks literacy's connections to power, to social identity, and to ideologies, often in the service of privileging certain types of literacies and certain types of people. (Gee, 1996, p. 46)

Difficulties with the Pluralist View

The suggestion that there could be many literacies is an unsettling one for educators. Teacher training courses and textbooks rarely acknowledge it as a possibility or a problem. This is especially so perhaps in early childhood education where teachers have been drawn to individual psychological models of development. Difficult questions are raised by the pluralist view. If there are different literacies, is there any justification for valuing some more than others? Which literacy should be taught, and why? What if the child's home literacy is different from the school's literacy?

There is certainly a problem here for teachers who wish to respect families' language and literacy and who do not want uncritically to impose school literacy on them. However, teachers' business is school literacy and it would be self-deceiving to imagine that under current schooling arrangements all families' literacies can be accepted as a substitute for school literacy. For many families, involvement in the teaching of literacy is bound to mean being involved in new and different forms of literacy. For example, the narrative fiction genre is very prominent in texts used in the early years in school but, as Heath (1983) showed, some families are not familiar with using written language in this way. Other examples might be essay writing, poetry, reading nineteenth-century fiction. Promoting school literacy in such families runs the risk of importing – maybe even subtly *imposing* – new uses for written language. This may be difficult to achieve since it usually has to be attempted without changing or extending the cultural context which supports the existing pattern of uses for written language in families. If it is successful the result may be to distance children from their families. Yet, not to do anything or simply reflecting back and facilitating the family's existing uses for literacy, may simply reinforce children's exclusion from school and whatever benefits school success confers.

Specific information, rather than generalities, may help us understand in what ways the two literacies are congruent or divergent, and the nature of parents' aspirations. All social action involves dilemmas but it is better to be aware of their nature than have them hidden. Working at the home–school literacy boundary is both rewarding and uncomfortable since it means having a critical awareness of two worlds of literacy, both of which have value but neither of which can be accepted wholly or uncritically. Research findings by themselves will not resolve the dilemma of whose literacy we are to promote but research may bring the issues into sharper focus and provide us with concepts for thinking out courses of action and with a vocabulary for dialogue with parents.

In addition to educational and political problems raised by the pluralist view there is a theoretical problem in that as soon as one begins to subdivide the field of literacy into different literacies it is hard to know where to stop. Barton (1994) shows how, within one or two pages of a local newspaper, it is possible to distinguish a wide range of literacies. They include legal notices, concert advertisements, personal advertisements and publicity for a health club. These are all written in slightly different ways, assuming different knowledge on the part of readers. It would be very odd indeed if one encountered advertisements for a rock concert written in the style of a local government legal notices but is it useful to refer to these as *different literacies*? Where does it end? With a little more effort one could probably discern different styles of concert advertisements, even different styles of rock concert advertisements. To refer to them all as instances of different literacies seems to push the concept beyond the limits of usefulness.

Another problem is that the boundaries between different literacies may not be as easy to draw in practice as they are in theory. Barton and Hamilton (1998), for example, explain that they found 'the distinction between the home and other domains is less clear-cut than we first imagined'.

> At first we imagined we would encounter a distinct home literacy which could be contrasted with work literacy or school literacy. To some extent this is true. There is a distinctiveness to many home literacy practices, but what is more striking is the range of different literacies which are carried out in the home, including work and school literacies which are brought home where they mingle together. (Barton and Hamilton, 1998, p. 188)

Thus the pluralist view – that there are literacies – has to struggle with the twin difficulties of being unsure about how far to go in enumerating different literacies and being unclear about distinguishing one literacy from another.

Reconciling Different Views of Literacy

A common dilemma facing researchers and theorists in many fields of enquiry is deciding whether the most efficient conceptualisation is to consider a range of cases as instances of different concepts or as different instances of a single concept. It is necessary to create a set of concepts which balance the requirement to distinguish particularities with the requirement to recognise generalities. In thinking about literacy in education both requirements have to be met. The pluralist view, in distinguishing different literacies, provides powerful insights but runs the risk of making it difficult to see the whole. The unitary view facilitates consideration of literacy as a whole but overlooks its contextual variation, particularly in relation to power structures in society.

In searching for a reconciliation between the unitary and plural views it may help to acknowledge that, even if there are many different literacies, it does not follow that they are all *completely* different. One is reminded of Wittgenstein's (1953) examination of the concept of a 'game' – a concept not unlike literacy in apparently encompassing a wide variety of different activities. Wittgenstein pointed out that diversity need not prevent us categorising the activities together.

> And the result of this examination is: we see a complicated network of similarities overlapping and criss-crossing: sometimes overall similarities, sometimes similarities of detail. I can think of no better expression to characterize these similarities than 'family resemblances' for the various resemblances between members of a family: build, features, colour of eyes, gait, temperament, etc. overlap and criss-cross in the same way. And I shall say 'games' form a family. (Wittgenstein, 1953, sections 66, 67)

Perhaps it would be helpful to characterise literacy practices as a 'family' of social practices where there may be considerable overlaps and similarities between some instances (e.g. reading postcards from friends and reading and emails from them) whereas others may be only distantly related (e.g. writing poetry and completing a driving licence application).

Because there are many branches of literacy it does not follow that there is no tree. There may be significant overlaps between apparently different literacies or core processes common to many literacy activities, especially in the early stages of learning them. Appreciating that written English is a way of representing the sound structure of spoken English, knowing how to translate text into speech and vice versa, being aware that the use of upper case letters can be significant, that texts have authors, that revision can improve writing, that there are different genres, that punctuation marks serve a different function from letters are all examples of knowledge that can play a part in many literacy practices. Appreciating that : -) in an email message is shorthand for 'take this humorously' is an example of knowledge presently restricted to one kind of literacy

Literacy is not the only concept with a tension between generality and particularity. Consider 'music' – a concept which covers an enormous range of activities in many cultures. Some forms of music seem utterly different in terms of technology, conventions and purposes from other forms. Yet we do not find it necessary to assert that there is a plurality of 'musics'. That would only be necessary if some group in society asserted that only their form counted as music and what others did was not music at all. Other concepts which could be considered in the same way include 'money', 'love' or 'language'.

In the case of 'language', it often suits our purposes to acknowledge that there are many languages – English, Mandarin, Spanish, Xhosa, and so on. One can acknowledge that American English is not the same as British English and that even within Britain there are varieties of English. One can also acknowledge differences between social groups or classes within the same locality in terms of speech conventions, vocabularies, accents and predispositions to use language for different purposes. However, none of this prevents use of the word 'language' to refer to things which transcend the particular instances – the evolution of language, its development in children, the inevitability of grammar.

I suggest that theorists' taste for unitary or pluralist conceptions of literacy derives from whether their primary focus is on literacy as skill or on literacy as social practice. The two foci are traditionally associated with psychology and sociology respectively. *Table 1* summarises features of each. Where the focus is on literacy as skill, literacy is likely to be viewed as unitary. This is not to suggest that it is seen as involving only one skill. It is likely to be seen as involving a complex set of closely interrelated skills ranging from the grapho-phonic to the cultural. A 'core' or 'basic' set of skills may be sufficient for dealing with a

Table 1:   Different conceptions of literacy

Skills-focused	Practice-focused
Unitary view likely ('literacy')	Plural view likely ('literacies')
Acquisition seen as result of individual learning	Acquisition seen as result of social involvement
Learning seen as transferable	Learning seen as context-dependent
Literacy may be measurable	Literacy not quantifiable
Literacy relatively fixed	Literacy continually changing
Literacy intrinsically value-free	Literacy inevitably value-laden

wider range of instances of written language use but it is acknowledged that new skills may be needed for certain purposes. A high degree of transferability is assumed (e.g. some of the skills involved in writing a fictional story may be applied to writing a scientific report). Skills-focused theorists may well be open to the idea that skill levels can be measured and they tend not to be overly concerned with the social processes which make some skills more valued than others. Practice-focused theorists do not have much interest in skills (and may even reject the very idea of skills) preferring instead to emphasise socio-linguistic practices in their accounts of literacy. For them questions of context and power are extremely important.

How do we choose between these different conceptions? Perhaps it is not necessary to choose. We can have both. I suggest that too narrow a focus on either 'skill' or 'practice' results in an inadequate account of literacy. To focus on skill without acknowledging that skill can only be evidenced in being exercised in social practices (and that it involves a continually developing *repertoire* of skills) would seem to be absurd. Likewise, emphasising social practice to the extent of denying that skill acquisition of some kind is required, seems equally absurd. Skill and social practice are not opposite conceptions of literacy but complementary perspectives. A full conception of literacy in education requires awareness of both. The desire to understand literacy is sometimes best served by focusing on the many different ways in which written language is used within social groups to achieve a variety of purposes but at other times it makes more sense to focus on the commonalities, particularly in how literacy is acquired.

One researcher who appears to have tried to integrate both conceptions is Concha Delgado-Gaitan (1990).

> The abililty to interpret linguistinc and graphic symbols associated with text requires one type of ability. Literacy is a sociocultural process, and it follows that another literate ability has to do with the sociocultural knowledge and cognitive skills that are necessary for the child and the family to interpret text. (Delgado-Gaitan, 1990, p. 29)

Like other polarities in literacy, 'one literacy versus many' turns out to be too gross a simplification of the processes we are trying to understand.

Reflecting on School Literacy

How should all this affect how we think about literacy in education? If we recognise that literacy is a social practice, and that it varies according to the purposes of people in different social contexts, the nature and content of literacy promoted by schools (which for shorthand can be called 'school literacy') becomes more than the imparting of skills.

It is not all that easy to provide a complete description of school literacy. Official curriculum and policy documents tell part of the story but, of course, there can be a gap between curriculum intentions and what actually happens in practice. The hidden curriculum is, by its nature, even harder to fathom. There is a need for descriptive research studies of the daily literacy experiences of pupils in classrooms, corridors and playgrounds. Ideally studies would cover pupils of different backgrounds in all age levels of the education. Some such studies have been carried out but so far they provide a very incomplete picture. Many are restricted to classroom lessons in English (Wragg et al., 1998; Webster et al., 1996).

In England much of school literacy is described in the English subject National Curriculum Orders (now augmented, at primary level, by the *National Literacy Strategy: Framework for Teaching* document: DfEE, 1998). In addition there are the literacy requirements of other subjects such as report writing in science or note making in history. Literacy is also part of the hidden curriculum, for example in the reading of school signs and documents or using a writing task as a form of punishment.

The *National Literacy Strategy Framework for Teaching* (DfEE, 1998) gives an explicit definition of the literacy it seeks to promote by stating that 'literate primary pupils should':

- read and write with confidence, fluency and understanding;
- be able to orchestrate a full range of reading cues (phonic, graphic, syntactic, contextual) to monitor their reading and correct their own mistakes;
- understand the sound and spelling system and use this to read and spell accurately;
- have fluent and legible handwriting;
- have an interest in words and their meanings and a growing vocabulary;
- know, understand and be able to write in a range of genres in fiction and poetry, and understand and be familiar with some of the ways in which narratives are structured through basic literary ideas of setting, character and plot;
- understand, use and be able to write a range of non-fiction texts;
- plan, draft, revise and edit their own writing;
- have a suitable technical vocabulary through which to understand and discuss their reading and writing;
- be interested in books, read with enjoyment and evaluate and justify their preferences;
- through reading and writing, develop their powers of imagination, inventiveness and critical awareness. (DfEE, 1998, p. 3)

The focus here appears to be more on the acquisition of skills than on the engagement in social practices but it is hard to see how the former can succeed without the latter. The challenge for teachers is to find or contrive opportunities for engagement in literacy practices as a means to acquiring skills.

Investigating what school literacy *is* leads on to some interesting questions about what it *should* be. The act of describing school literacy itself requires some view about what is or should be important in it. Also, once school literacy is described, it is natural to ask whether it is what we want, and to compare it to home literacy, community literacy, workplace literacy and so on.

School literacy is the outcome of action taken over a long period by certain groups in society including agencies of the state, elected governments, local education authorities, schools, and individual teachers. For most of the twentieth century in Britain the state allowed schools or local education authorities to define school literacy through locally created curricula. Recently, however, the literacy curriculum has been subject to extremely tight central control. I do not wish here to discuss at what level (state, area, school or classroom) the content of school literacy should be decided, or by whom, beyond expressing the hope that it be done as democratically as possible at whatever level it is done. Rather, I want to discuss the principles which govern, or could govern, what counts as school literacy.

There are at least seven principles which might be considered: (1) family choice; (2) workforce requirements; (3) social differentiation; (4) equal opportunities; (5) personal development; (6) citizenship; (7) social change. These are not all necessarily mutually exclusive but initially they can be considered singly.

1   *Family choice* One principle might be that school literacy should consist of whatever families want – no more and no less. Parents could be asked what they wanted their children to be able to do. They might be presented with a list of possible literacy practices (including, say, 'understanding Shakespeare', 'following household appliance instruction manuals', 'writing poetry', 'writing letters of complaint') and be asked to indicate which they wanted their children to be able to engage in. In addition they could be asked whether they wanted their children to acquire whatever literacy was necessary to achieve other ends such as examination passes in various subjects (it could be left to teachers to work out what that entailed for particular subjects in terms of essay writing, note taking, reporting, and so on). As children grow older they might be expected to take a larger part in the family decision. Such a 'pick and mix' literacy curriculum presents three major problems for families. One is that families many not be able to make informed choices about what they want, especially if the parents' own literacy repertoire is limited. Uninformed choices could mean families excluding children from educational opportunities and the perpetuation of educational and social inequalities. A second problem is that the rest of society also has an interest in what should be expected from school leavers. Third, 'pick and mix' is usually impractical. It is too difficult to disassemble school literacy and then parcel it up in different combinations for different pupils. In any case, most families would probably opt for an 'off the shelf'

curriculum package provided that it appeared to be reasonably coherent, that it reflected some professional consensus and that it was likely to maximise children's educational and employment opportunities.

If families do not define what is school literacy, it becomes more important to make explicit the principles by which others might decide what it should be.

2 *Workforce requirements* There is no doubt that the current reformulations of school literacy – relating to both what should be taught as well as to how it should be taught – owe much to what are thought to be the demands of working life. Yet this too would seem to be an inadequate basis for defining school literacy. In the first place, it is far from clear what are the literacy demands of various jobs. To determine these is in itself a major research task. The workforce is stratified so there would be a question of which set of literacy demands should be anticipated in the case of particular school leavers. Also, of course, under the pressure of change in information and communication technology, literacy demands are continually changing – particularly rapidly at the present time – so that preparing children for the literacy demands of today's jobs may leave them ill equipped for tomorrow's jobs. Finally, to allow the world of work entirely to shape school literacy would mean submitting to a narrowly utilitarian view of the purposes of education.

3 *Social differentiation* The society which school leavers enter is stratified. Schools will not by themselves change this. Powerful groups benefiting from current inequalities may see it as the function of schools to fit children into appropriate strata in a manner which they will accept and that school literacy may have a role to play here in securing their acquiesence. If school literacy is defined so as to reflect the literacy practices of powerful groups in society, and if children's success in these practices is regularly assessed, then children may come to accept school achievement as a measure of their entitlement to rewards in society.

4 *Equal opportunities* One could argue that schools should seek some redistribution of life chances of pupils by deliberately initiating them into the literacy practices of the more powerful. The nature of different genres should be laid bare for children to see and to grasp. This would be a principle whereby school literacy could be shaped (and indeed has motivated the initiatives of genre theorists in some educational systems such as Australia).

5 *Personal development* One might consider promoting literacy in school with the aim of enhancing the personal development of all pupils. This presupposes that there is some way of judging what kind of personal development is valuable. One has to be careful

here that opening doors for children to engage with certain aspects of literacy (e.g. reading nineteenth century novels) does not become a way of asserting the preferred literacy practices of the powerful as the norm to which all should aspire. Even to promote some revolutionary uses of literacy (e.g. encouraging working class children to write poetry about *their* experiences of life) has to rest on someone's – often the teacher's – idea of what is right for pupils.

6   *Citizenship* One could try to work out what kind of literacy in school would best support the kind of society we wish to have. Your desired society may not be the same as mine but almost any imaginable society has expectations of its new citizens, and if it uses written language at all there will be a literacy aspect to these expectations. This could be the basis for defining school literacy.

7   *Social change* It could be that education is seen as a tool for transforming society – a means of bringing about social change. This goes beyond principle (4) which concerns equality of opportunity to a more radical concern with altering the pattern of opportunities within a society. Socialist educators might take this position. The teaching approach of Paulo Friere, discussed in Chapter 5, was intended not only to enable peasants to read but also to increase their understanding of their oppression and their engagement in revolutionary struggle.

These seven kinds of principles for shaping school literacy do not exhaust all the possibilities. Some groups in society, for example, may wish religious principles to shape school literacy. Various combinations of principles are possible too. It is interesting to speculate on what principles may have led to the aims for school literacy quoted earlier from the *National Literacy Strategy: Framework for Teaching*. The point here, however, is not to seek a justification of current school literacy or some reformulation of it in the future. That is a political and philosophical enterprise beyond the scope of this book. Rather my aim is to bring to the fore some key considerations which are bound to be part of defining school literacy. Behind every assertion about what literacy should be taught in schools and how it should be taught there are assumptions – often unspoken – about the importance or the irrelevance of the kinds of principles discussed above. School literacy is not a given but something which is the outcome of particular social and political forces at a moment in history. We fail to understand the nature of literacy if we think otherwise.

Further Reading

In trying to identify readings which inform the issue of whether there is one literacy or many, it is difficult to identify proponents from different sides of a debate.

Those who engage most explicitly with the issue are those who wish to argue strongly for plurality. Those who assume a unitary view tend either to be unaware of the issue or choose not to make their assumptions explicit. Nevertheless these three sources are worth examining.

BARTON, D. and HAMILTON, M. (1998) *Local Literacies: Reading and Writing in One Community*, London: Routledge. This book is a careful ethnographic investigation of literacy practices in one town in the north of England. David Barton and Mary Hamilton identify what they term 'vernacular literacies, or local literacies, in people's everyday lives'. Their book provides strong theoretical and empirical support for the 'many literacies' position.

DEPARTMENT FOR EDUCATION AND EMPLOYMENT (1998) *The National Literacy Strategy: Framework for Teaching*, London: DfEE. This document details literacy learning objectives for primary school children in England. Read it to understand a close-of-century official view of school literacy and ask, 'What principles underpin its definition of school literacy?'

TAYLOR, D. (Ed) (1997) *Many Families, Many Literacies: An International Declaration of Principles*, Portsmouth, NH: Heinemann. This book is an international collection of over 60 extremely diverse contributions to understanding literacy in families and to understanding the educational implications, particularly for family literacy programmes. Implicitly and explicitly the contributors mount a strong case for recognising and celebrating plurality.

Chapter 4

Theories of Literacy Development

Overview

This chapter introduces some key theoretical issues concerning literacy development in children and adults. After reflecting on what is meant by 'literacy development', and why it is worth trying to theorise about it, two main theoretical perspectives are discussed. One focuses on the development of individuals' engagement in the literacy practices of the social groups in which they participate. The other perspective focuses on the development of skills which are necessary for those literacy practices. A conceptual framework which attempts to accommodate both perspectives is proposed.

The Idea of Literacy Development

Literacy development can be defined as the process in which children (or, in some circumstances, adults) change from being totally unable to use written language to being able to use it in one or more contexts. One could refer to this change simply as 'learning' but, from a psychological perspective, the term 'development' is helpful in that it suggests parallels with cognitive development, language development or social development where the learning is complex, involves the organisation and successive reorganisation of skills, often following a sequence, and may be characterised by qualitative as well as incremental changes. Most cognitive developmental theories in psychology acknowledge that the individual has an active role in constructing that development. Closely connected to the idea of development is the idea that there are developmental norms within social groups but that various constitutional or environmental factors can promote or impede development.

Child development is the outcome of interaction between environmental factors (including cultural ones) and inherent characteristics of the child. Some aspects of development (e.g. sensori-motor abilities) appear to be relatively unaffected by cultural factors – as least across the range of cultural variation likely to be familiar to readers of this book. Even language development, despite being deeply cultural, appears to have substantially similar characteristics across known societies. Literacy development, however, varies enormously across cultures as might be expected from the discussion in the previous chapter of the 'many literacies' thesis. In literacy the cultural factors include teaching whether that is carried out within or outside educational institutions.

All this makes the very concept of literacy development problematic. Literacy is so much the outcome of culture and teaching that it is not clear what regularities in the sequencing, rate, nature or end point of learning it is reasonable to expect across cultures. On the other hand it is not unreasonable to expect *some* regularity. There may be many 'pathways' to literacy but some may be better trodden or easier to follow than others and some cross-country routes may be well nigh impossible.

'Nothing so Practical as a Good Theory'

The above maxim, sometimes attributed to the psychologist Kurt Lewin, challenges the prejudice that there is a conflict between theory and practice, that they pull in opposite directions and cannot help each other. It is a reminder that there are very often practical motives for devising theories. Most practical action is based on theory of some kind even if that theory is not explicitly stated. If the theory is wrong, however, and if it is never made explicit, practice is bound to suffer. It is certainly possible to carry on teaching reading and writing without being theoretically aware. One could even, on the surface, appear quite competent at it. I would argue, however, that this is not good enough.

We need theory – for at least four reasons. First, theory helps satisfy our professional curiosity about the processes of learning and teaching literacy which we see in our everyday work. Not to be curious about such things would imply a worrying detachment or alienation from one's work. Such curiosity is one motivation which leads teachers to study on advanced courses. Second, we can look to theory to help practice. Theory enables us to choose, on some rational basis, which approach to take in teaching situations. Third, theory enables us to grow professionally. The alternative is to carry on doing things the same way throughout our entire careers or to change merely on the basis of educational fashion, whim, or someone else's orders. Fourth, theory enables us to explain what we are doing to children, students, parents, and the wider public. Not being able to explain renders teachers vulnerable to outsiders who 'know better'.

The Social Practice Perspective on Literacy Development

In the previous chapter a view of literacy as social practice was put forward. If one accepts that view the challenge for developmental theory is to explain how children come to understand and participate in the literacy practices of the groups and institutions in which they find themselves. Initially this is likely to be their families; later it may be their schools.

One theoretical perspective which has been enormously influential in providing concepts for thinking about this is due to Vygotsky (1896–1934), a Russian psychologist whose work was suppressed in the Stalinist era but which became enormously influential many years afterwards following publication in English

(Vygotsky, 1978, 1986; Daniels, 1993). Vygotsky was anxious to relate the development of internal psychological processes within the individual to wider social processes. One consequence of this approach was that he distinguished children's developmental level in terms of what they could do on their own from their level in terms of what they could do in co-operation with other members of society. He coined the unwieldy, but still valuable term, *the zone of proximal development* to refer to the range between these two levels.

> The zone of proximal development defines those functions that have not yet matured but are in the process of maturation, functions that will mature tomorrow but are currently in an embryonic state. These functions could be termed the 'buds' or 'flowers' of development rather than the 'fruits' of development. The actual developmental level characterises mental development retrospectively, while the zone of proximal development characterizes mental development prospectively.
>
> . . . what is in the zone of proximal development today will be the actual developmental level tomorrow. (Vygotsky, 1978, pp. 86–7)

This has implications for understanding what kind of interaction might be most appropriate for children learning to read and write. From Vygotsky's point of view it should *not* be limited to a child's current level but should extend and challenge the child.

> What the child can do in co-operation today he can do alone tomorrow. Therefore the only good kind of instruction is that which marches ahead of development and leads it; it must be aimed not so much at the ripe as at the ripening functions. (Vygotsky, 1986, p. 188)

From the adult's point of view, the challenge is to interact with learners in ways which balance the need to challenge and extend them with the need also to support them so that they remain engaged in meaningful and successful activity.

Frank Smith (1988) has used the metaphor of 'joining the literacy club' to characterise the social nature of literacy learning. He argues that children develop literacy by joining a community of readers and writers who use literacy to accomplish real purposes. The established members of the club (including the authors children encounter) draw the new members into their activities. They do not expect children to learn everything at once so they help them with things they cannot do in the confident expectation that eventually they will be able to join in all club activities. Smith suggests that this is the only way children can learn effectively—there being 'no evidence that any child ever learned to read by simply being subjected to a program of systematic instruction'. The metaphor is persuasive and Smith urges teachers 'to ensure that clubs exist and that no child is excluded from them' by providing a wider range of classroom activities. This points to an appropriate form of interaction between teacher and child being closer to the expert–apprentice relationship rather than the instructor–pupil relationship.

Here it may be helpful to consider parallels between oral language and written language. These are connected in that the acquisition of written language nearly always depends on the prior acquisition of oral language. Looking for parallels does not mean ignoring obvious and important differences between oral and written language. However, it is worth reflecting on how children learn each kind of language, and the nature of adult–child interaction in each.

Children's early attempts at speech are generally taken seriously by parents who tolerate imprecision and errors and do their best to interpret what the child means – even at the babbling stage. Adults often structure situations to make it easy for children to understand and make themselves understood. Might such assistance and encouragement be just as valuable in the development of reading and writing – from the stages of earliest 'scribbling' stage and puzzling out the meaning of texts? Children learn to understand speech by making sense of meaningful communication – of varying levels of complexity – in natural contexts so that although adults sometimes simplify their speech for children's sake, they do not always do so. Children do not usually have to undergo direct instruction in understanding speech. We do not have to expose them to utterances of graded complexity (by having a language programme of some kind) but it is often assumed that this is necessary for learning to read. One could characterise children's learning of spoken language as being 'on the job' – in natural contexts, as required. It is reasonable to suppose that their learning to understand written language could be similarly facilitated in shared reading of books and other texts to achieve clearly understood and shared purposes such as the enjoyment of narrative. Margaret Meek (1982) has put it this way:

> Reading is whole-task learning right from the start. From first to last the child should be invited to behave like a reader, and those who want to help him should assume that he can learn, and will learn, just as happened when he began to talk. . . . Learning to read in the early stages, like everything else a child has come to know, is an approximation of adult behaviour with genuine meaningful function. (Meek, 1982, p. 24)

In so far as there are significant similarities between the development of children's spoken and written language it means taking seriously the fact that children could learn from a range of uncontrolled encounters with written language (many outside the school context), that such encounters need to be as meaningful as possible, and that parents as well as teachers are bound to have a key role in mediating them.

However, there are also differences between written and spoken language. For example, a writer cannot take it for granted that his or her reader will share the same context in the way that a speaker can often assume that a hearer does (indeed written language is more likely to be used when the two are *not* in the same context). This means that the character of written language often differs significantly from spoken language in being less context-dependent – more explicit and self-contained – than much speech (and is therefore rarely 'speech written down'). Children who are unfamiliar with using oral language in this way may find this difficult to grasp. It should also be noted that at the level of psychological processing there are fundamental differences between written and oral language use and acquisition. For example, as Reid (1993) has pointed out, there appears to be no innate capacity for acquisition in the former as there is in the latter and there is no significant similarity between early speech utterances and samples of early writing (which are more like transcriptions of mature utterances).

Nevertheless it is worth noting that in the normal development of spoken language the ability to produce speech is intimately connected with the ability to understand it. It may be just as helpful to recognise the links between reading and writing but it often happens that these two are treated as separate processes. The concept of *literacy* unites them.

The Skills Perspective on Literacy Development

Few would dispute that literacy involves a vast number of interrelated skills. This is not necessarily to assume that the skills have any existence separate from the activities in which they are exercised. It has been assumed by some educationists, however, that certain skills have to be acquired *in order to* learn to read and write. In reading these have often been referred to as pre-reading skills which children have to be taught explicitly. Some years ago Walker (1975), for example, argued that 'success in the skills of reading depend on successful acquisition of the related subskills of prereading' (p. 7) and,

> In order to overcome the unique difficulties inherent in beginning reading it is necessary for the child to have *first* developed a minimum set of skills and capacities. (Walker, 1975, p. 20, emphasis added)

The skills in question were thought to be mainly perceptual (shape and letter discrimination, hand–eye coordination, left–right eye movements, visual memory, listening and auditory skills, phonemic discrimination, auditory memory, letter recognition, knowledge of letter names and sounds). In writing, the important skills were thought to include drawing, copying and remembering basic shapes and letters.

The difficulty here is to identify which skills are really important as prerequisites. Although certain skills are found in proficient readers and writers, it is possible that they are acquired *as a result* of learning to read and write rather than as a prerequisite for such learning. Learning to ride a bicycle, for example, involves many skills (such as aspects of balancing, steering, pedalling) but it would be very difficult to teach someone to ride by teaching them the sub-skills and then expecting them to be proficient riders. It is much more likely that the skill is learnt as a whole, and specific skills are acquired as a part of that whole (what, in the previous section, Margaret Meek called 'whole-task learning'). Therefore one has to look rather carefully at claims that this or that specific skill is necessary for the acquisition of literacy.

On the other hand there do seem to be certain skills or knowledge which, if not absolute pre-requisites, are extremely helpful. Here are some which have been highlighted by research into literacy development.

Research by Gordon Wells in Bristol and Barbara Tizard and colleagues in London has highlighted the importance of children's *knowledge of literacy at school entry* (Wells, 1987; Tizard, et al., 1988, Tizard, 1993). In the Wells study children were given Marie Clay's *Concepts of Print* test which reveals their understanding of books and text and they were also asked to name as many letters of the alphabet as they could. Wells (1987) found a 'very strong relationship between knowledge of literacy at age 5 and all later assessments of school achievement' (p. 147). Similarly, in the Tizard studies the strongest predictor of reading attainment around age 7 was letter identification just before age 5. It is likely that this kind of knowledge *in itself* is not the crucial factor but that it is a good indicator of a range of preschool literacy experiences.

The crucial factor according to Wells (1985, 1987), who examined data from his longitudinal study, is children's experience of stories in the early years:

> because stories are self-contextualising, sustained symbolic representations of possible worlds, they provide the child with the opportunity to learn some of the essential characteristics of written language. Reading and discussing stories helps the child to cope with the more disembedded uses of spoken language that the school curriculum demands. (Wells, 1985, p. 253)

Catherine Snow has argued for the importance of a closely related aspect of oral language – children's experience of *de-contextualised talk* (Snow, 1991). Like Wells she believes that children need familiarity with uses of language which are common in written language – especially in school – but which may not be part of all children's preschool oral language experience.

Phonological and phonemic awareness are other skills identified by researchers as important. In Chapter 2 it was pointed out that writing is a way of representing oral language (or at least selected features of oral language). There are several features of oral language which carry meanings – pitch, amplitude, prosody, intonation – but it is the sounds we are able to make by channelling and stopping the flow of air through our mouths that are perhaps the most important and, in the English writing system, it is these sounds which are represented. It follows that awareness of the sound structure of English is very important for literacy development. The precise nature and role of sound-awareness is not yet fully understood and it is a hotly contested area of research with, as we shall see in the next chapter, major implications for how literacy should be taught. Some researchers focus on children's ability to recognise similarities in word endings ('rhymes') and similarities in the beginning sounds of words ('onsets') and refer to this as 'phonological awareness' (Goswami and Bryant, 1990). One way in which young children can acquire phonological awareness is through nursery rhymes and it has been found that the number of nursery rhymes which a child knows at age three is a good predictor of their reading and spelling attainment at age six, even when other factors such as social class have been controlled (Bryant et al., 1989). There are other sound units which can be considered too. In English there are probably 44 (some say 43) phonemes. These are the smallest units of sound which, in terms of their absence or presence, distinguish words from one another. For example the phoneme /b/ is the sound which, substituted for the phoneme /k/, changes 'cat' to 'bat'. Some researchers argue that it is awareness of phonemes which is the key factor in literacy development (Byrne, 1998; Nation and Hulme, 1997). Measures of children's awareness of phonemes in the early school years are good predictors of reading ability later in school. However, as it is not easy to measure phonemic awareness before children are taught literacy there must be some doubt as to whether phonemic (as opposed to phonological) awareness is a cause or consequence of early literacy development. Also, phonological awareness probably gives readers other advantages in reading and writing (Goswami, 1999).

Cognitive Perspectives on Literacy Development

One of the major perspectives on learning in the twentieth century, Piaget's theory of cognitive development (Piaget and Inhelder, 1969), is associated with a distinctive perspective on literacy (Goodman, 1990b). The key idea here is that the literacy learner is regarded as actively trying to make sense of his or her encounters with written language rather than just being the passive recipient of external influences. To appreciate learners' achievements one has to make careful observations of their early attempts to read and write. In one classic study from this perspective, *Literacy before Schooling*, Ferreiro and Teberosky (1982), for example, showed that preschool children realise at an early age that writing carries meaning but it is a challenge for them to understand that whereas the meaning of a picture depends on the objects that it refers to, the meaning of writing is the *words* that it refers to.

Vygotsky suggested that writing required the development of an explicit knowledge of the sounds and grammar of a language which helps 'the child rise to a higher level of speech development' (Vygotsky, 1962, p. 101). He further argued that writing demands abstraction – of two kinds. The first is at the level of psychological processes.

> Written speech is a separate linguistic function, differing from oral speech in both structure and mode of functioning. Even its minimal development requires a high level of abstraction. It is speech in thought and image only, lacking the musical, expressive, intonational qualities of oral speech. In learning to write, the child must disengage himself from the sensory aspect of speech and replace words by images of words. (Vygotsky, 1962, pp. 98–9)

The second kind of abstraction arises from the fact that writing, unlike speech, cannot be part of a dynamic social situation such as a conversation and therefore has to be more consciously directed by the child.

The motives for writing are more abstract, more intellectualised, further removed from immediate needs. In written speech we are obliged to create the situation, to represent it to ourselves. This demands detachment from the actual situation. (Vygotsky, 1962, p. 99)

This analysis shows how literacy development is intertwined with other strands of intellectual development.

An influential theory of learning in psychology for a large part of the twentieth century was behaviourism. There have been several varieties but common to all has been a concern to explain learning in terms of associations between observable events (stimuli, responses, behaviour) at the level of the individual and without reference to unobservables such as meaning or intention. In reading, this has meant a concentration on how learners come to recognise words or parts of words through some stimulus–response process. For example, reading programmes such as 'look and say' based on teaching the recognition of whole words through simple texts, flashcards and other means are behaviourist in this sense (although they may have been informed by other perspectives, such as Gestalt theory, too). Some phonic-based programmes that set out to teach grapheme-sound correspondences directly can also be regarded as behaviourist. What matters according to this approach is arranging children's experiences so that they can learn one set of words (e.g. the most important, the most frequently used, the most memorable, the simpler phonically, and so on) before moving on to the next set.

The kind of interaction considered important from the behaviourist perspective is that which: directs children's attention to the important stimuli (e.g. words or parts of words); presents learning material in carefully graded stages; requires success at one stage before moving on to the next; matches tasks to the child's level of development; generates behaviour (e.g. through repetition, games, exercises); and reinforces or rewards correct responses. There is no doubt that this approach does focus on important aspects of literacy learning and interaction. But it also ignores some important ones. There is very little concern with the *purposes* of literacy or with the *meaning* of what is read or written.

When people are asked to think about their definition of reading and writing they often want to include a reference to *meaning*, e.g. 'reading is getting the meaning of a text'. It does not seem sufficient to define reading only in terms of knowing which words in oral language are associated with which bits of print. No one reads merely to decode text. It follows that appropriate interaction in learning to read is interaction which will help novice readers get the meaning of what they are reading and, more than that, will help them see that reading *is fundamentally about* deriving meaning.

One influential theoretical approach which emphasises the importance of meaning has been miscue analysis. This was originated in the 1960s by Kenneth Goodman who argued that children's errors in reading could reveal the psychological processes involved, and to emphasise that errors were not random but indicative of underlying strategies he referred to them as 'miscues' (Goodman, 1969). In her book, *Listening to Children Reading,* Helen Arnold (1982) offered a simplified form of miscue analysis which can be carried out under classroom conditions by teachers. Children are tape-recorded reading to the teacher from any passage of 150–300 words, difficult enough to 'tax' but not frustrate the child. Afterwards (presumably not in class time) the teacher examines the recording to note and code the occurrence of eight kinds of miscues – non-responses (refusals), omissions, insertions, repetitions, reversals (of words), hesitations, self-corrections and substitutions. The last of these, substitutions, are considered to be particularly revealing and are examined further to see whether they have grapho-phonic, syntactic or semantic similarities to the original. Arnold suggests that miscues can be 'positive' or 'negative', broadly according to whether or not they indicate the child is attempting to read for meaning. Therefore one aim of the miscue analysis is to establish the overall balance between the 'positive' and 'negative'.

The diagnosis can have some implications for interaction. Arnold (1982) suggests that from miscue analysis the teacher can identify which strategies a child needs to develop in order to make progress. A poor reader, with many 'negative' miscues, might need to be encouraged to use meaning to overcome difficulties, for example through detailed discussion of the text with the teacher. There may of course be other reasons why teachers should employ miscue analysis: a basic one being that it may sensitise them to ways in which all readers learn and therefore to the most helpful kind of teacher–pupil interaction to promote literacy development.

Stage Theories of Literacy Development

Developmental theorists in all areas of psychology have fondness for delineating the stages through which children pass in the course of development. Sometimes this is little more than the naming of parts; in other cases the characterisation of stages is such that it provides some kind of explanation of the dynamics of movement from one stage to the next.

In the area of reading, Jean Chall (1983) proposed a six-stage framework as follows.

1   Pre-reading (development of oral language and awareness of literacy)
2   Learning to read (using letter-sound associations to understand text)
3   Extending early reading (extension of skills with accessible texts)
4   Reading to learn the new (reading beyond own area of experience)
5   Reading multiple viewpoints (reading to understand others' viewpoints)
6   Construction and reconstruction (reading to form one's own views)

Chall argued that each of these stages were distinguishable and that they constituted a logical hierarchy in that the five 'school level' stages were each dependent upon the child reaching the preceding stage. One can accept this for stages 1–3 but it becomes less clear thereafter. Also, it is difficult to avoid feeling that there is something prescriptive – rather than descriptive – about the higher stages. They may represent aspirations for teachers but they may not be the way things turn out for many children. Nevertheless, as Beard (1990) suggests, provided that the stages are not regarded as too definite and fixed, this framework may have some value in structuring discussion about the reading curriculum.

Of more interest from a developmental viewpoint is a three-stage theory proposed by Uta Frith (1985). First, in the 'logographic' stage of reading, children may have sight vocabularies of dozens of words which they are able to recognise as wholes. With the right kind of support children move into the 'alphabetic' stage in which they learn about the relation of parts of words to the sounds of oral language. This permits decoding of new words but that may be a rather slow process until increasing familiarity with the spelling system permits more rapid word recognition in what Frith (1985) terms the 'orthographic' stage.

The danger with stage theories is that they overlook two important considerations in development. The first is that literacy development cannot be likened to biological maturation which, given basic environmental conditions, proceeds through regular stages. Literacy is essentially cultural and literacy development is therefore bound to reflect the cultural arrangements made for inducting new members of a group into the group's literacy practices. In short, literacy development is shaped by literacy teaching. There may be some logical or cognitive constraints which prevent certain developmental routes being followed but many pathways still remain. For example, one could imagine a culture in which children were denied experience of written words until they knew basic phoneme–grapheme correspondences. In such an (unusual) context they would not be likely to exhibit Frith's logographic stage.

Second, implicit in the concept of 'development' is the metaphor of linearity. There is the suggestion that development proceeds in a sequence, A leading to B, to C and so on. Yet even in the social contexts familiar to readers of this book there may be several developmental routes open to children depending upon chance variations in their family and school circumstances. This has led some authors to search for other metaphors. Trevor Cairney (1995), for example, refers to 'pathways'.

> One of the clearest lessons that I have learned in my 25 years as an educator is that there is no single pathway to literacy learning. Indeed, there are probably as many pathways as there are literacy learners, because we all learn to be literate in rich social contexts as we engage in unique sets of human relationships. (Cairney, 1995, p. ix)

In similar vein, Yetta Goodman (1997) asserts,

> There is no single road to becoming literate. As I read the work of those who have studied the literacy development of children in many places in the world, as I consider the kids (my own children and grandchildren among them) who have informed my literacy development research, I am convinced that it is extremely important to legitimise the concept of multiple roads to literacy. (Goodman, 1997, p. 56)

While acknowledging that children do learn to read as a result of officially recommended experiences such as being read to and following published curricula, Goodman goes on to identify other 'roads' such as the 'writing road', the 'survival road', the 'playing-at-literacy road', 'environmental print road' and the 'technological road'.

It appears that in this area of child development, the attempt to map preferred pathways, roads or highways is likely to be frustrated by the sheer variety of social contexts in which children's development takes place. We may have to settle for a looser characterisation of development

The ORIM Framework

An implication of a social practice perspective for understanding literacy development is that theories of literacy development which refer only to the individual learner are somewhat suspect. Equally, social practice theories which treat individual learning as unproblematic or unimportant are rather unsatisfying. Development is the result of the interplay of cultural/social processes and individual/psychological ones. Ideally we need an overall view which somehow embraces both sets of processes. One attempt to do this is the *ORIM* framework which has grown out of work at the University of Sheffield (Hannon et al.,1991; Hannon, 1995; Hannon and Nutbrown, 1997). *ORIM* is an acronym which refers to four probable requirements for literacy development – *opportunities* for literacy learning, *recognition* by others of one's learning achievements, appropriate *interaction* with users of written language, and a *model* of literacy use. To consider what these mean, consider first literacy development in the early childhood years, then in the later years (see box).

In the early years, parents can provide vital learning *opportunities*: by resourcing children's drawing or scribbling activities; by encouraging their socio-dramatic play; by exposing them to, and helping them interpret, environmental print; by teaching nursery rhymes which aid speech segmentation and phonological awareness; by sharing story books and other written materials; and by enabling children to participate in visits, trips or holidays which provide further literacy demands and opportunities. Parents can provide unique encouragement for children in their *recognition* and valuing of children's early achievements

> **Some requirements for literacy development**
>
> Opportunities
>
> Recognition
>
> Interaction
>
> Model

in, for example, handling books, reading, understanding logos, and writing. They need to *interact* with children – supporting, explaining and challenging them to move on from what they know about literacy to do more. An important way of doing this is to involve children in real literacy tasks in which they can make a meaningful contribution (e.g. adding their 'name' to a greetings card, turning the pages of a book) thereby enabling to do today with an adult what tomorrow they will be able to do independently. Some parents deliberately teach their children some aspects of literacy. Finally parents act as powerful *models* if and when children see them using literacy, for example, in reading newspapers for information or enjoyment; writing notes or shopping lists; using print to find things out, to follow instructions; or to earn a living, for example, by bringing work home.

It is also helpful, for practical reasons, to distinguish different strands of literacy development. In the early years these could be children's experiences of *reading* (environmental print as well as books and other texts), of *writing*, and of *oral language* (to include storytelling, phonological awareness, de-contextualised talk). These are represented in *Figure 1*.

For each strand of literacy, children need opportunities, recognition, interaction and a model. In *Figure 2* each cell in the matrix refers to an aspect of parental support for literacy (e.g. providing a reading model, appropriate interaction in writing). The value of the framework is that it can be used to describe how particular families support children's literacy development but it can also be used to plan curricula or work with parents. One can ask in relation to each cell in the matrix, 'What can we do here to improve children's experiences?'

Figure 1: Some strands of early literacy

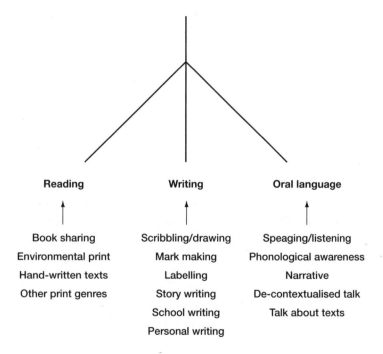

Reading	Writing	Oral language
Book sharing	Scribbling/drawing	Speaging/listening
Environmental print	Mark making	Phonological awareness
Hand-written texts	Labelling	Narrative
Other print genres	Story writing	De-contextualised talk
	School writing	Talk about texts
	Personal writing	

Figure 2: A framework for viewing literacy development

Strands of literacy experience

	Reading	Writing	Oral language
Opportunities			
Recognition			
Interaction			
Model			

What learners need

In the later years, children need the same things but possibly provided in different ways. School obviously becomes much more important. Providing literacy *opportunities* in school means having many rich and varied activities and resources and, outside school, it may mean facilitating children's use of libraries or creating reading time for them (for example, by limiting TV viewing). It may mean providing resources such as dictionaries, encyclopedias, magazines, newspapers, books, writing material or even computers. *Recognition* of achievement means teachers and parents appreciating children's reading and writing more difficult texts at home and in school. Appropriate *interaction* in the form of talking about books, newspaper articles or writing tasks continues to be very significant. As in the early years, it could take the form of direct instruction. Providing a *model* of literacy goes beyond merely being seen to read and write to a clearer demonstration of how these activities are linked to a wide range of adult purposes in the home, community and workplace.

The *ORIM* framework was originally developed as a way of developing practice in the field of parental involvement in the teaching of literacy before school but it has wider applicability in understanding literacy learning in other contexts (and probably in understanding other kinds of learning). It can be applied to adult literacy development – not just to the development of adults who have difficulties but also, for example, to those of us who read and write in universities – whether as students, teachers or researchers.

At university level the strands of literacy which matter differ somewhat from those of importance at the preschool level. They might include the following.

Reading	Using libraries
	Skimming textbooks
	Reading research articles
	Understanding tables of research findings
Writing	Writing essays
	Making notes
	Using writing to develop one's ideas
	Devising efficient personal filing systems
	Correspondence with one's tutor
Oral language	Giving seminar presentations
	Asking questions

Postgraduate students will have no difficulty adding to this list.

Whatever the relevant strands of literacy for each of us, if our literacy is to develop we are likely to need opportunities, recognition, interaction and a model. Masters' courses in education generally aim to provide some of these. For example, there will be *opportunities* for reading research texts through the materials provided and opportunities for writing in essays and in preparation for seminars and tutorials. There is some *recognition* of students' reading and of writing in feedback on assignments. *Interaction* occurs in tutor–student communication and student–student exchanges. As to *models*, the most powerful will be the authors of the readings provided and the authors students discover for themselves during the course. Authors obviously provide a model of writing but they also provide a model of reading in the way in which they draw on the work of others.

The *ORIM* framework is just one way of looking at development which emerged in the work of one research group at a particular time and place. To put it in a wider context it needs to be appraised critically by looking at its strengths and weakness, at what it covers and at what it overlooks. Among critical questions to be asked of it are the following.

How clear and understandable are the key concepts (opportunities, recognition, interaction, model, literacy 'strands')? Does the framework really assist understanding of children's literacy development? Could the framework be applied to teaching pupils or students? Does the framework make sense applied to post-school literacy development? What developmental issues does it overlook? The framework is reasonably clear and helpful *as far as it goes* but the main problem is with the concept of 'interaction' – it is very broad and imprecise. One could say that any reasonable theory of literacy development ought to tell us *what kinds* of interaction lead to what kinds of outcomes and merely stipulating that there needs to be some interaction does not take us very far. Another limitation is that the framework does not help us understand the development of skills and processes within the individual learner (e.g. the role of phonological awareness in word recognition, how we learn to spell, the nature of dyslexia, and so on). The framework is more to do with the context (particularly the social context) within which development takes place rather than what exactly is learned in the course of that development. However, it does suggest that skills learning can take place within that overall context.

It would be satisfying to have an overall theory of literacy development which explained how all the relevant internal processes linked with social ones. Unfortunately, that is unlikely to happen for some time yet because if such a theory existed it would mean that some of the most fundamental problems in perception, neurology, psychology, philosophy, and social/cultural studies would have been solved. The best we can hope for is theories which illuminate parts of the overall picture.

Conclusion: Becoming Theoretically Aware

This chapter has managed only to scratch the surface of the topic of literacy development. Some of the issues and ideas will recur in the next chapter on teaching methods. Meanwhile I would like to suggest that we should strive to be aware that there is a *range* of useful theories of development and, although it is natural to want to have just one, in the present state of knowledge we need to resist the temptation of adopting any one theory as the *only* acceptable way of understanding development.

Further Reading

BEARD, R. (1990) *Developing Reading 3–13* (2nd edn), London: Hodder and Stoughton. This book remains a useful source of information regarding different perspectives on literacy development. As might be guessed from the title, its emphasis is on how literacy is developed (i.e. literacy teaching) and as such it is also relevant to the following chapter, 'Teaching methods'.

FERREIRO, E. and TEBEROSKY, A. (1982) *Literacy before Schooling*, Portsmouth, NH: Heinemann. This was an early attempt to map development from a Piagetian perspective. Although it is not wholly convincing from that point of view, this study revealed the child's constructive effort in understanding literacy and paved the way for the 'emergent literacy' perspective.

GOSWAMI, U., and BRYANT, P. (1990) *Phonological Skills and Learning to Read*, Hove: Lawrence Erlbaum. This landmark study reports and reviews research into the development of children's awareness of the sound structure of oral language and its written representation. Although restricted to one aspect of literacy development, the analysis of evidence remains a model of how psychologists can contribute to an overall understanding of how children become literate.

HALL, N. (1987) *The Emergence of Literacy*, London: Hodder and Stoughton. This book is an excellent summary of the emergent literacy perspective on early development. This perspective has been very influential in revealing the extent of literacy learning which is independent or prior to literacy teaching.

Chapter 5

Reflecting on Teaching Methods

> The theorising mind tends always to the over-simplification of its materials. That is the root of all that absolutism and one-sided dogmatism by which both philosophy and religion have been infested. Let us not fall immediately into a one-sided view of our subject. (William James)

Overview

Although William James (1960, p. 46) was not referring to the teaching of literacy, his comments apply perfectly to views held on that subject. For many people how it should be taught is *the* most important question concerning literacy in education. While it is certainly *an* important issue we have seen in earlier chapters that there are others, too, such as defining goals in teaching literacy, deciding what should be in the literacy curriculum, and having some understanding of how individuals can develop literacy. In judging which teaching methods are most valuable we have to keep an eye on all these interconnected issues. It is because proponents of particular teaching methods not only express views about method but also inevitably make assumptions about the purpose of literacy, the goals of education and the nature of human development that this topic has the potential to arouse so much controversy. To avoid 'over-simplification' and 'dogmatism' it is necessary to acknowledge complexity and uncertainty and to recognise truths in different views as well as errors.

Some writers who have been dismayed by the extreme views in debates in this field have called for balanced approaches (Beard, 1993; Bielby, 1998; Pressley, 1998). This is an understandable response but the metaphor of 'balance' may not fully reflect what they are striving for in so far as it suggests that one should aspire to be midway between extremes. That would mean one's position being liable to be shifted one way or another by extreme views advocated at the fringes. Also, there may be some issues on which one should not budge. It is preferable to develop one's view of teaching methods on the basis of principles, accepting what seems to be valuable in various methods according to those principles. One relevant priciple concerns *evidence*. This does not help us choose between methods if they relate to completely different teaching situations or if the conflict between them is really about different goals but whenever differences can be narrowed down to a question which can be answered empirically then those who claim the superiority of one method over another should be called upon to provide evidence. That is one way of avoiding a 'one-sided view of our subject'. The aim of this chapter is to introduce some ideas and principles which may help us reflect upon methods of literacy teaching.

Comparing Teaching Methods

It is important to note at the outset that the teaching of literacy can take many forms, each varying in several ways. The same word 'teaching' can be used to refer to one-to-one teaching situations in the home or in a clinic as well at to situations where there is one teacher to thirty or more learners in a classroom and where the learners may be as young as 5 or 6 years old. What the 'teacher' does in these situations is very different. What is possible and desirable in one situation is impossible in another; what is a necessity in one is undesirable or unnecessary in the other. In small groups such as families it is possible for learners to be initiated slowly and individually into literacy practices whereas in large groups an emphasis on imparting discrete skills to all learners at the same time may be the only way teachers feel they can make progress. It would be naive to assume that family teaching methods could be transplanted unaltered into classrooms or vice versa. The theory of learning or the theory of literacy development most applicable to the teaching practice is likely to vary according to the situation, e.g. in terms of the importance given to making learning activities being meaningful versus learning by rote. There are also variations in terms of how far the teaching of reading is integrated with the teaching of writing. There are variations in the concept of literacy which it is the aim of the teaching to impart. There is the issue of how deliberate is the teaching – at one extreme there can be systematic, planned instruction and at the other simply the provision of opportunities whereby learners can construct their own literacy in a social context.

In addition to these variations most teaching methods also vary in which aspect or level of literacy they prioritise. We can conceptualise being literate as being able to deal with all the following levels of written language – usually simultaneously.

Levels of literacy which can be the focus of teaching

  1   Purpose
  2   Text
  3   Sentence
  4   Word
  5   Sub-word

Most teaching methods concentrate on teaching input in just one or two of these levels. For example approaches which insist that children are taught phoneme awareness and phoneme–grapheme correspondences before anything else are giving priority to level 5. At the other extreme would be total reliance on engagement with storybooks – focusing on levels 1 and 2. Few would dispute, however, that in the end users of written language need competence at *all* levels.

When one considers how many permutations of all these variations are possible it becomes clear that simply to talk about 'the teaching of literacy' is not adequate. One needs to talk in plurals – about the 'teachings of literacies'. Nevertheless what has happened in the development of teaching methods, and in the controversies they engender, is a tendency to focus narrowly on certain situations and certain levels of literacy to the exclusion of others. Sometimes this may be on the grounds that if one level is secured, the others can easily be added. Hence advocates of 'whole language' teaching methods may focus on the upper levels in the belief that awareness and use of phonic regularities in reading and writing is something that will follow later as a result of the learner's own activity. Advocates of phonics often show little practical interest in whether children enjoy reading or appreciate the purposes of writing, believing that these are unproblematic once 'the basics' are secured.

What is it to *Teach* Literacy?

Let us reflect on the nature of 'teaching' and how it relates to 'learning'. Teaching is not always necessary for learning to occur (and even when teaching seems to be necessary a very small amount can sometimes result in considerable learning). We know this from our own life experiences – outside as well as inside formal educational settings – where we learn many things which no one has really taught us. Teachers with several years' experience, for example, usually feel that they have learned a considerable amount about their job but this is not because they have been *taught* everything (in fact they are often critical of how little they have ever been taught). Professional learning comes about from having the right kind of opportunities, recognition of one's successes, stimulating interaction with colleagues, and teachers who serve as good models to emulate. Some theories of literacy development already discussed in the previous chapter place great emphasis on this kind of learning by pointing to the capacity of young children to make sense of the world of print which surrounds them and thereby to learn literate aspects of culture without much obvious teaching. For example, Yetta Goodman has argued that 'the development of knowledge about print embedded in environmental settings is the beginning of reading development, which in most cases goes unnoticed' (Goodman, 1986, p. 7) Emilia Ferreiro and Anna Teberosky, basing their investigations of children's literacy learning on Piagetian ideas, concluded:

> In a field where it has been thought, in spite of a variety of viewpoints, that learning cannot take place without specific instruction, and where the learner's contribution has been thought to depend on and derive from the instructional methods, we have discovered a developmental line in which cognitive conflicts play an essential role. (Ferreiro and Teberosky, 1982, p. 285)

Margaret Meek's suggestion that children learn through active involvement in real literacy activities is summed up in the title of her monograph *How Texts*

Teach What Readers Learn (Meek, 1988). From these perspectives there appears to be very little teaching going on. We might say that learning is the result of the individual's interaction with the environment. Of course, in the case of literacy the environment is a *social* one in which others are producing and using written language for various purposes, sometimes in activities which involve the learner. Goodman, Ferreiro and Teberosky and Meek share a strong implicit concern with social interaction in learning literacy. They take it for granted that those who are more proficient in the use of written language are often willing to help others – particularly children – who are still learning. Should we call such help 'teaching'? Perhaps, but we need to recognise that if there is teaching here – even if it is powerful – it is conducted in an intermittent and unobtrusive manner, to be characterised perhaps in terms of the *ORIM* framework discussed in the previous chapter. I suggest that such teaching be termed *facilitation*.

Often, however, the word 'teaching' implies a more deliberate and sustained attempt to shape another's learning. I suggest this be referred to as *instruction* – teaching which is explicit and planned, with clear aims and objectives and where experiences are provided for learners so as to maximise the probability of certain outcomes. Instruction can be carried out formally or informally but in either case it is purposive and governed by teaching aims. Instructional teaching episodes are likely to be timetabled over a long period. Activities and experiences are organised for learners in such a way that they learn what is required as quickly and as efficiently as possible. The teacher decides on the optimum order for learning experiences and plans instruction accordingly. Irrelevant experiences are treated as distractions and excluded as far as possible. Instruction can be carried out with groups or individuals but is more common with groups, notably in class teaching where it is impracticable for teachers to provide the individual interaction with learners which characterise facilitation.

Compared to instruction, *facilitation* is a less intensive form of teaching and tends to be embedded in other (often everyday) activities. It is opportunistic – more patient and less urgent than instruction. It can still be deliberate – even if the teaching aims are at the edge of the teacher's consciousness. Teachers are aware of desirable learning outcomes even if they rarely plan teaching episodes to achieve specific objectives. The teacher, seeing the opportunity to impart some knowledge, might temporarily take on a teaching role before resuming an earlier one. Teaching episodes may be brief and relatively spontaneous. The teacher is open to unexpected learning and may be willing to follow the learner's interests. Facilitation can be very powerful for individual learners because it relates to their immediate concerns. For the same reason it is less suitable for groups of learners.

Which is better, instruction or facilitation? Both have had their advocates. For example, in the 1970s Herbert Kohl argued that learning to read needed the kind of facilitation that works for learning to talk, and that methods of teaching reading employed in schools were counter-productive.

If talking and walking were taught in most schools we might end up with as many mutes and cripples as we now have non-readers. However, learning to read is no more difficult than learning to walk or talk. The skill can be acquired in a natural and informal manner and in a variety of settings ranging from school to home to streets. (Kohl, 1974, p. 9)

In the 1980s, Margaret Meek expressed a similar view in terms quoted in Chapter 4.

Reading is whole-task learning right from the start. From first to last the child should be invited to behave like a reader, and those who want to help him should assume that he can learn, and will learn, just as happened when he began to talk . . . Learning to read in the early stages, like everything else a child has come to know, is an approximation of adult behaviour with genuine meaningful function. (Meek, 1982, p. 24)

More recently, however, opposite views of what kind of teaching is necessary have come to the fore. One example would be this claim by Diane McGuinness:

Reading is skilled behaviour and, like all skills, it has to be taught from the bottom up, from the simple parts to the complex whole. No one would dream of asking a novice diver to attempt a difficult dive like a reverse jacknife. Nor would one teach a beginning piano student to use all ten fingers at the first piano lesson. All skilled learning builds piece by piece, through practice, until the skills are integrated. (McGuinness, 1998, p. 17)

It is interesting to note the analogies chosen by these proponents. Meek and Kohl invite us to see the teaching of literacy as like the facilitation involved in helping a child learn to talk or walk; McGuinness prefers to compare it to the instruction involved in teaching high diving or piano playing.

How are we to decide between these different conceptions? First, it is helpful to entertain the possibility that there is some truth in both conceptions (however unwelcome such a thought might be to the above authors). We need to recognise that the phrase 'teaching of literacy' refers to many aspects of literacy, to many different learners at different ages, and to many learning situations. Learning to walk or talk is perhaps an appropriate analogy for some learners, learning some aspects of literacy, at some times. At other times, in other contexts, at least some learners could benefit from instruction. Neither analogy has to be accepted as applicable to all cases, all of the time. Second, instruction and facilitation need not be irreconcilable types of teaching. It might be more productive to think of mixing them in varying proportions according to need – of there being a *teaching spectrum* with instruction at one end and facilitation at the other. Literacy teaching in school (usually with one teacher to many learners) tends to be at the instruction end of the spectrum whereas teaching at home (or in any context where learners do not greatly outnumber teachers) is likely to be closer to facilitation.

Thinking about literacy teaching in this way, and accepting that it can mean more than one thing, helps us, in a fiercely contested area, to avoid false polarities between different methods.

The Initial Teaching of Literacy

The teaching of literacy must have just as long a history as literacy itself but most of that history is obscure. Perhaps when literacy was restricted to a few individuals in society, and 'on the job' learning was feasible for most learners, teaching consisted mainly of facilitation and was regarded as no more problematic than the teaching of many other skills. On the other hand there is evidence from as far back as the Sumerian period of quite formal schooling (A. Robinson, 1995). What is fairly clear is that as mass schooling developed in modern times so did the need for explicit teaching methods and, by virtue of the teacher–pupil ratio in schools, this meant a need for instructional methods.

Pre-twentieth century methods of teaching reading appear to have involved what is often called the *alphabetic method*. To teachers in the past there probably seemed no alternative method and they would probably not have applied any kind of label to it. In essence it meant teaching children the names of letters of the alphabet ('ay', 'bee', 'cee', etc.) and then getting them to use this knowledge to decode words. Obviously, as a decoding strategy this had its limitations. Letter names do contain phonemes which the letters represent on *some* occasions (e.g. the letter name 'd' in 'dog') but often a letter represents phonemes not in the letter names (e.g. the letter name for 'c' gives no clue to what sound that letter represents in 'cat'). This does not mean teachers of previous eras were misguided, less intelligent or less resourceful than those of today. All teachers have to match their methods to available physical and cultural resources. In any case it is likely that the basic alphabetic method was supplemented by teaching further letter–sound associations (e.g., letter 'a' says 'ah', letter 'b' says 'buh', and so on) which would have given children more clues to the pronunciation of many words. From the later Middle Ages it became common for children to use 'hornbooks' (actually not books at all but so called because a thin sheet of horn was used to cover and protect writing on parchment attached to a small wooden board). Hornbooks displayed the letters of the alphabet in upper and lower case, a few common syllables and the text of prayers which children would already have known by heart (the 'sign of the cross' and the 'Lord's Prayer'). One can imagine how teachers could have used hornbooks in a variety of exercises to teach reading and writing.

With advances in technology, including the production of paper and printing, and consequent changes in pedagogy, the alphabetic method became more elaborated. Michael (1993) describes how in the seventeenth and eighteenth centuries some teachers paid more attention to spelling, sometimes putting it before reading. In the second half of the nineteenth century and the early decades of the twentieth century, more explicit 'phonic' methods were developed (Beard, 1990). These involved children working through books with highly controlled – and often rather meaningless – texts.

Thus for many centuries methods of initial teaching focused on the 'sub-word' level of literacy. The use of known words within prayers on hornbooks suggest some concern with the word level too but in the mid-twentieth century this level for a while became the main focus in the *whole-word* method. This method, inspired by a desire to make early reading as meaningful as possible, and influenced by ideas from Gestalt psychology that words could be perceived as wholes, meant teaching children to recognise individual words through flashcards and other means. Whole-word methods usually involved a controlled introduction of words which resulted in some rather contrived texts. Many children did learn to read in this way with minimal teaching about sub-word letter–sound relationships. The fact that they were later able to read new words suggested that they learned to spot similarities between unknown and known words or that they had inferred some letter–sound relationships. Nevertheless explicit teaching of letter–sound relationships was thought unnecessary until children's reading was quite developed or until it was clear that they were experiencing difficulties.

Sub-word methods never went away. Rather than being 'alphabetic', however, they became *phonic*, that is based on a fuller analysis of the relationships between sounds in language and specific letters or combinations of letters. Most phonic methods involved presenting children with letters or letter combinations and teaching them the corresponding sounds, i.e. the direction of teaching could be said to be from letters to sounds. Children were taught to blend sounds together, eventually to form words. This approach is sometimes termed *synthetic phonics* in that words are synthesised out of constituent sounds. It can be contrasted with *analytic phonics* in which children are taught letter–sound relationships by analysing how parts of words contribute to their pronunciation. Although proponents of different phonics methods draw a sharp distinction between these two approaches, even asserting that they are mutually exclusive, in practice the two have often coexisted, sometimes within single teaching interventions by teachers.

One feature common to both phonics methods and whole-word methods from the 1950s to the 1970s was control of the order and difficulty of texts encountered by children. In the UK this was through ordered sets of books comprising 'reading schemes'; in the US there were more elaborate 'basal reading programs' which included additional reading and writing resources. The texts which children encountered was often very stilted prose and purposeless which gave them an experience of reading at odds with what teachers hoped they would eventually come to enjoy. It must have been a particularly dreary experience for children who were slow to learn, especially if they had few stimulating literacy experiences at home. In the same period, outside schools, there was a dramatic increase in the amount and quality of books published commercially for children. This was due to a combination of technological advance in colour printing and book production, the growth of a mass market of families with income to spend on their young children, and the emergence of committed authors and publishing houses intent on providing for young children some of the reading pleasures familiar to adults. The contrast between texts genuinely written for children and those contrived for instructional purposes was too much for many teachers to bear. Also, they noticed that many children were learning to read through the former which became known – for purposes of polemic – as 'real books'. In the 1980s reading schemes were extensively supplemented, complemented or replaced by 'real books' and teachers relaxed their control somewhat over the order of text difficulty. Publishers of reading schemes became generally very sensitive to criticisms on this point and anxious to claim literary quality for the texts they put before children.

The critique of reading schemes and programs went beyond dissatisfaction with the quality of text offered to children. In the UK, the 'real books' movement, and in the US, the 'whole language' movement challenged basic assumptions about literacy instruction in schools. Drawing on some of the ideas about literacy development discussed in the previous chapter, it was argued that just as children's oral language development did not depend upon exposure to carefully graded learning experiences neither should their reading development. It was argued that school instruction took no account of the fact that children were growing up in a print environment before school, and out of school, and that they were actively constructing their knowledge of it. It was argued that it was inappropriate to treat young learners as empty vessels passively waiting to be filled. Instructional methods also treated reading and writing separately, often reducing the latter to technical skill rather than attempting to embed it in communicative activity. In other words, it was argued that there should be much more of a focus on the higher levels of literacy distinguished earlier – purpose and text levels rather than sub-word and word levels.

The initial teaching of literacy has not yet reached a settled state. Perhaps it will always be in flux. As one method or focus becomes dominant a new generation of younger teachers begins to question its assumptions. As soon as that generation has reached positions of power which enables it to implement alternative ideas another generation has entered the scene and begins the process anew. This would be one explanation for why the period of oscillation of swings in teaching methods is roughly the time, twenty to thirty years, it takes for a generation of new teachers to reach positions of influence and decision making. In England, in the late 1990s, the initial teaching of literacy is being determined by the National Literacy Strategy which can be seen as a reaction to an earlier consensus. But even as the new methods become established one can surmise that the Strategy is creating the conditions for an opposite reaction around 2025 if not before.

The Phonics Revival

In the late 1990s in Britain there were renewed attempts by proponents of phonics to promote their methods (Davies and Ritchie, 1998; Lloyd, 1998; D. McGuinness, 1998; C. McGuinness and G. McGuinness, 1998; Miskin, 1997). Although there were differences between the various methods advocated, a common feature was the emphasis given to the phonemic level in language and an insistence that early learning of phoneme–grapheme relationships was the key to later success in reading and writing. To understand some of the issues raised by the phonics revival we can take one example – the case put forward by Diane McGuinness in her book, *Why Children Can't Read* (1998). This is worth examining in some detail because it is recent and because it is a determined, systematic and forcefully expressed contribution to current debates.

McGuinness concedes that traditional phonics methods were often unsatisfactory because of the arbitrary and confusing nature of rules taught to children for decoding words into sounds. She argues that it is too much to expect children to learn different sounds for the hundreds of different letter combinations found in written English. She argues that is misleading to suggest to children that they have to learn any more sounds beyond the forty-four (or, according to her, forty-three) phonemes in the English language. For example, the word ending '-unch' is not a single sound but a blend of three separable phonemes, /u/+/n/+/ch/ and it is more economical to learn the constituents than the (more numerous) combinations. For McGuinness initial teaching should not be about moving from letters to sounds (as in the old alphabetic and some phonic methods) but going in the opposite direction from sounds to letters. Children should first be taught to identify and produce all the English phonemes and then shown that there is a logical way of representing them in letters in words.

McGuinness asserts that there is such a thing as a 'true logic of the English alphabet code' (1998, p. 98) and that it can be taught to literacy learners through a carefully designed instructional programme. It is a common claim of phonics methods that they provide children with a key to unlock words. To define her code for instructional purposes, McGuinness says that she analysed three thousand common English words in terms of all the different ways in which phonemes were represented by letters. Some ways of representing particular phonemes were more common than others. For example, the consonant phoneme /h/ was more often encoded as 'h' (as in 'hot') than as 'wh' (as in 'whole'). For teaching purposes one can start with the most common representations of each phoneme. McGuinness refers to this as a 'Basic Code'. In many cases a single letter can be the code for a phoneme but as there are only twenty-six letters in the alphabet some phonemes have to be represented by digraphs (two letters for one sound), e.g. 'ch', 'aw'. Also, to distinguish different phonemes represented by the same letters, underlining or overlining is used (e.g. the consonants beginning the words 'thing' and 'them' are represented as 'th' and '<u>th</u>' respectively). This is certainly a code and it is also logical in that there is a one-to-one correspondence between all phonemes and their written representation. In principle it could be used to write any word in spoken English, albeit with unconventional spellings.

In this method learners are taught the 'Basic Code' by teachers who are themselves familiar with the phonemes of spoken English and how they can be encoded into words. Children are first taught to produce phonemes orally and then taught to say words associated with various pictures (e.g. cat, ball, dog). All words at this stage are CVC (consonant + vowel + consonant) so that each part of the word is a single phoneme. Children are asked to group pictures on the basis of the initial phoneme of each word, then the last phoneme, and finally the middle one. Once learners can distinguish phonemes sufficiently well to group pictures they are taught that each phoneme in a word can be represented by its own 'sound picture' (a card showing the relevant letter or letters in the 'Basic Code').

There are exercises in using letters to encode phonemes in different positions in words (including nonsense words), in segmenting, in blending and in distinguishing vowels from consonants. Digraphs are dealt with only after single letter representation of phonemes have been mastered. 'Chaining' exercises in which children move from one spoken word (or nonsense word) to another by changing, removing or adding phonemes one at a time, are also used to teach segmenting and blending. Learners are taught to copy letter shapes but children are not allowed to 'waste classroom time' in scribbling, colouring, or writing letter strings not legitimate in English spelling. Letter names, upper case letters and cursive handwriting are not allowed. Traditional children's literature is 'off limits' because it has too many irregular spellings.

When they know the 'Basic Code' learners are able to read a restricted number of words but of course they are a long way from being able to read ordinary written English. The next stage according to McGuinness is to teach them an 'Advanced Code'. Here it is acknowledged that phonemes can be encoded into more than one grapheme. Some phonemes have just one grapheme (e.g. /d/ is always represented by 'd') but most have alternatives. For example, the /i/ sound can be represented by 'i' in 'it', by 'y' in 'baby' or by 'ui' in 'circuit'. McGuinness suggests that these are explained to learners as 'spelling alternatives'. According to her, there are some 135 phoneme–grapheme correspondences for 43 phonemes. In the 'Advanced Code' some graphemes are shared by different phonemes, e.g. the letter 'o' can represent the phoneme /oe/ as in 'go' or the phoneme /o/ as in dog. McGuinness refers to these as 'overlaps'.

Learning the 'Advanced Code' means learning the various alternatives for encoding phonemes and learning that some are more likely than others. McGuinness specifies sequences for teaching the alternatives for initial consonants, initial consonant clusters, final consonants, and vowels. The 'code overlaps' are taught through sorting games and exercises using words where different phonemes are represented by the same grapheme. Children are also taught to segment multisyllable words into syllables, and to segment syllables into phonemes. McGuinness has devised special spelling 'dictionaries' in which the correct spelling of common words can be found by looking them up according to their sounds. Learning to read and write, for McGuinness, is being able to use the 'Advanced Code'.

McGuinness's approach claims to build on the strengths, and learn from some of the weaknesses, of previous phonic approaches. It is very definite about the nature of written language in relation to spoken language. Key ideas are developed and followed through into practice, sometimes quite ingeniously and she is optimistic about the capacities of learners and what they can achieve. There are, however, some problems with the approach which illustrate difficulties shared by other phonics methods.

Although McGuinness's 'Basic Code' has some plausibility as a code there are serious problems with the so-called 'Advanced Code'. It is extraordinarily complex. Not only does it involve learning a large number of phoneme–grapheme associations (135) but it stretches the concept of a code to breaking point by allowing one-to-many correspondences, between what is to be encoded (phonemes) and the code elements (letters/graphemes). The one-to-many corre-spondences occur in both directions. The complexity is such that the same grapheme can be implicated in one-to-many correspondences in both directions, i.e. not only as one of a number of possible encodings of a phoneme but also with a possible decoding into a different phoneme. For example, there are no rules to tell learners which alternative grapheme to use in encoding phonemes into words nor any rules to specify which phonemes should be decoded from particular graphemes in words. At best the 'Advanced Code' indicates that there is a finite number of possibilities (and the relative likelihood of each possibility is another thing to be learned). All this may help learners but it is a long way from having a code. The reasons why a particular phoneme–grapheme correspondence is con-ventionally correct often makes sense to experts familiar with the long history of English orthography but for most learners the correspondences will seem arbi-trary, without any logical basis. This is a code without a key. A further problem occurs with words whose encoding cannot be accounted for at all in the 'Advanced Code'. McGuinness claims: 'there are less than fifty of these in com-mon English words' (1998, p. 103). She does not say how she arrived at this figure but presumably it is fifty out of the sample of three thousand common words she analysed. Unfortunately there is no explanation of how that sample was selected except that it did not include the 'Latin layer' of the English language. Many words with Latin endings lie outside the 'code' and have to be learned separately. It is therefore possible that learners could encounter many words which do not conform to the 'Advanced Code'. Taking all these problems together the 'true logic of the English alphabet code' promised by McGuinness remains elusive.

McGuinness seems not have a consistent position on the power of visual mem-ory and associative learning. In discussing reasons why there is such a thing as an English alphabet she asserts that learners cannot possibly remember the written forms of all words – that it is simply beyond the limit of human memory. At other times she takes it for granted that learners can remember numerous alternative phoneme–grapheme associations and how they are employed in particular words. She suggests that repeated use of her 'sound dictionaries' increases familiarity with spellings of words so that the 'brain will begin to remember them without practice or conscious effort' (p. 276). She does not follow this logic through to the possibility that visual memory alone might be sufficient for proficient reading and writing and that, except when encountering completely new words, phoneme–grapheme knowledge may add comparatively little.

McGuinness's method seems not to be informed by any consideration of the end point of teaching. Teaching a 'code' cannot be an aim in itself for no one reads or writes simply for the pleasure of decoding or encoding. This is an exam-ple of a method which focuses on lower levels of literacy to the exclusion of the other levels. Literacy is actually about communicating and getting meaning through written language yet McGuinness never asks what implications this has for teaching. Months or years of rote learning using isolated letters, words and nonsense words could actually undermine long term goals of literacy teaching, especially for children who come to school with limited awareness of the uses of literacy. Also, psychological research indicates that proficient readers do not recognise words by decoding them phonemically but through visual recognition (Taft, 1991; Underwood and Batt, 1996). Visual recognition does involve attention to letters in words but that is quite a different matter from attending to phonemic encoding. Implicit in McGuinness's approach is an implausible model of word recognition in which readers scan letters in words from left to right, segment them into likely graphemes, permutate all the alternative phoneme decodings for each grapheme until they reach a combination which corresponds to the correct word. And how do they know when it is the correct word? Presumably by reference to a mental lexicon and contextual cues. A more likely process would be one of using visual features of a word to shortcut straight to the lexicon, eliminating unnecessary phoneme checking. If so, the aim should be to establish that lexicon and the use of context cues as soon as possible. If that is the main goal then perhaps teaching should discourage learners from becoming too reliant on phonemic level strategies and encourage visual recognition as early as possible. A clearer view of the learner's destination might affect how the journey is planned.

McGuinness is extremely hostile to alternative teaching methods and is adamant that they should never be combined with her own method. For example, she claims, without research evidence, that knowing letter names interferes with learning to read and spell. She insists on teaching only at the phoneme level even though there is evidence that knowledge of larger units of language, such as rhymes and their role in analogies, can be helpful (Goswami, 1999). Her absolutism regarding other methods presents her with a problem of how to explain the fact that many children who have never had the benefit of her method do in fact learn to read and write. She reviews survey evidence and argues that there are large numbers of poor readers in Britain and the United States but whatever way the figures are presented it is clear that most children in these countries do learn to read and write. She offers no explanation for this.

The dogmatism displayed by McGuinness is remarkable. Not mincing words, she states, 'There is only one right way to teach an alphabetic writing system' (1998, p. 221) and often refers to her method as the 'correct way'. She overstates the novelty of her insistence on moving from sounds to letters rather than the other way around (despite both directions being important).

Most of the questions raised so far could be settled empirically. Objections to the illogicality of the 'Advanced Code', the elimination of semantic and syntactic word attack strategies, the denial of authentic literacy experiences for children, and the tediousness of the training exercises would not amount to much if this method was actually hugely successful in practice. By 'success' could be meant enabling more children to learn to read and write with greater enjoyment, understanding and accuracy in comparison to what could be achieved with other approaches. McGuinness is keen on experimental evaluations of programmes. Such evaluations ought to be publicly available to the scientific community, preferably in peer-reviewed journals. She castigates those who advocate methods without evidence of effectiveness. It is therefore disappointing to say the least that no proper evidence is cited for the effectiveness of her methods in ordinary schools. Some evidence (from work with preschool children in private schools or failing readers in clinics) is put forward as to its *possible* value but there is no experimental study of the actual programme in practice.

This examination of the case put forward by one advocate of a phonics method reveals features common to advocates of many methods for the initial teaching of literacy. There is, first, a plausible rationale for some key ideas (in this case concerning giving children 'the code') but when these ideas are examined more closely they turn out to have more complexity and less generality than promised. Then there is a concern with one level of literacy (here the sub-word level) coupled with an implicit denial of the importance of other levels (e.g. text and purpose). There is absolutism and dogmatism in insisting on one true path to literacy and a distinct lack of research comparing the advocated method to other methods. It is necessary to be alert to these issues in the arguments made for all methods. Somehow we must find ways of rejecting overblown claims made for particular methods without losing sight of any valuable features they may have.

Parental Involvement and Family Literacy

An aspect of teaching literacy in school which has been significantly rethought in recent years is the involvement of parents. For most of the twentieth century the dominant practice in schools – at least in England – has been one of parental *exclusion*. Our present system of mass, compulsory schooling was set up – only four or five generations ago – with the specific design of taking children from their homes and parents for several hours a day in order to educate them in separate institutions. We have grown so used to this arrangement that it seems natural to us and we do not see how it is about excluding parents as well as educating their children. In the nineteenth century, when many parents were illiterate and schools were poorly staffed and overcrowded, exclusion may have been inevitable. However, a tradition was established then which was slow to reflect changing circumstances of an increasingly literate population and better resources. The 'professionalisation' of the teaching of literacy, especially the teaching of reading, is another factor in parental exclusion. Few areas of the curriculum have spawned so many techniques, technical terms, theories, books, tests, teaching materials, fashions or 'experts'. Reasons for this are not hard to find – literacy is a crucial component of the curriculum but its acquisition, as we have seen, is not well understood. Hence the confusion and complexity of teaching approaches. A professional vocabulary (including terms such as 'decoding', 'reading age', 'phonics') has emerged which can easily distance parents. There is also the feeling that 'if we find it so difficult to teach, then what hope is there for non-professionals like parents?'

Since the mid-1970s involvement has increased (or, one could say, exclusion has decreased). A turning point in England was the Plowden Report (Central Advisory Council for Education (CACE), 1967) which made recommendations for a minimal level of parental involvement in primary education. It concentrated on improving parents' understanding and school–home communication. From today's perspective, its suggestions may appear rather modest. Plowden had little to say about parental involvement in the teaching of literacy although it did establish a new climate in which significant innovation (e.g. in community education, in-school classroom parent involvement) could occur. However, for many years parental involvement in the curriculum remained rather limited – that is limited to relatively few parents (those able to come into school during the day), limited to children's in-school learning, and limited in the rather indirect role given to parents (covering library books or hearing selected children read in class under teacher supervision).

At the end of the 1970s the idea of direct parental involvement – focused on children's home literacy learning rather than their school learning – began to be explored. An enormously influential initiative was the Haringey Project which ran from 1976 to 1978. It was inspired by an earlier study reported by Hewison and Tizard (1980) which had found that a key factor in working class children's reading attainment at age 7 was how often parents hear their children read at home. Some did this regularly; others less often or not at all. What was significant about this finding was that it showed the importance of parents taking a *direct* role in children's literary development and that this seemed more important than many other factors (e.g. books in the home, parent–child language). The idea of the Haringey Project was to encourage *all* parents, rather than some, in a working class sample to hear their children read regularly at home. The results, reported later by Tizard et al. (1982), were very encouraging. The two-year involvement programme consisted basically of regularly sending reading books home with children and encouraging parents, through advice and home visits, to hear the children read. The reading test scores of project children at seven were much higher than those of comparable children not in the project. The later Belfield Reading Project, 1978–83, worked on similar lines to Haringey and despite less impressive results was also influential in providing a model for schools (Hannon and Jackson, 1987; Hannon, 1987).

The Belfield and Haringey projects took a fairly *open* approach to parents hearing children read – parents were given only the most general advice about how to do it. However, in the 1980s, some more *prescriptive* approaches were developed. Open approaches tended to be *comprehensive,* i.e. used for all children, albeit often in schools in disadvantaged areas. Prescriptive approaches were often *selective* (e.g. for older, failing readers) and *short duration* (weeks rather than months or years). The best known was *paired reading* in which parent and child read aloud and simultaneously (in a 'reading together mode') from a book chosen by the child. In paired reading the child has to try every word. If he or she makes a mistake the parent points it out, supplies the correct word and they read together without further discussion. If the child wishes to read alone ('the independent mode') he or she signals (e.g. by knocking on the table) and the parent stops. The child continues in the independent mode until a mistake is made, upon which the parent points it out, allows time for self-correction and if necessary gives the word. The reading together mode is then resumed, and so on. Throughout, parents are required to provide a stream of praise and to avoid criticism. Evaluations have shown paired reading to be consistently effective in short duration programmes (Bushell et al. 1982; Topping and Lindsay, 1991).

In practice, involvement can take many forms. The problem facing schools is not so much choosing one particular method as constructing their own from the many permutations of features which are possible. The typical age range for reading at home programmes is 5 to 7 but much will depend on the population served by the school. There is a major issue of whether a programme of involvement is for all children (comprehensive) or just for some (selective). The latter occurs when poorer readers are targeted but has the disadvantage of signalling to parents and children that involvement is only for those having difficulties. The objectives of involvement may be to improve specific aspects of literacy (e.g. enjoyment of books or reading test scores) but sometimes other objectives (e.g. improving home–school relations) are more important. Involvement may be seen as an integral ongoing part of school practice (i.e. with a duration of years) or as a short term intensive programme (a duration of weeks or months). The greatest variation lies in the method of involvement pursued. This is not just a matter of the focus and location of involvement but also of the assumptions which underlie open and prescriptive approaches to hearing reading.

There is much that we do not know – and need to research in the future – but what can be said with some certainty is that since the early 1980s there has been a momentous and probably irreversible shift in thinking about literacy at home and in school, and the role of parents in the teaching of literacy. It is now almost inconceivable that there could be a return to school-centred views of literacy as something children only learn as a result of being taught in school, of parents as marginal or even harmful in children's literacy development or of direct parental involvement in the teaching of literacy as impracticable or undesirable. We have learned that much literacy – perhaps most – is learned at home, that parents are central to that learning, that parental exclusion is unjustifiable, and that involvement is feasible, rewarding, and can help meet the goals of schools and families.

Teaching Methods with Adult Learners

It would be wrong, of course, to think of teaching methods just in terms of those used with children. Many adults seek to acquire literacy but the kind of teaching appropriate for them needs to be thought of quite differently. Adults usually come to the learning situation voluntarily, with much more experience of the world, with a clearer idea of what it is to be literate, and with some knowledge of their own learning styles. Therefore it is wrong uncritically to transpose teaching methods from children to adults.

One tradition of adult literacy teaching comes from initiatives to establish literacy in countries with relatively low levels of literacy in the population. In these circumstances the political implications of teaching of teaching methods cannot be ignored. There are well known examples from Latin America of literacy campaigns in the work of the Brazilian educator Paolo Freire (1970, 1972) and the Nicaraguan Literacy Crusade (Lankshear, 1987). These are examples of literacy for a specific purpose – that of the political struggle of oppressed groups. In the 1960s Freire developed a distinctive method of teaching literacy to adults (Brown, 1975). Exploiting the phonic regularities of written Portuguese, Freire's method was based on learning to read sixteen or so multisyllabic words which between them covered most of the grapheme--phoneme correspondences found in the language. Adults were shown how the words could be broken down into syllables which could then be recombined in various ways to form new words (or nonsense words). This technique, however, was subordinated to wider political and pedagogical values. The selection of the words came out of a long process of joint investigation between teachers and taught of 'themes' which were important in the lives of the taught. The words were highly charged (e.g. 'hunger', 'vote', 'illness', 'wealth') and were introduced in their written form only after their meanings had been extensively explored in discussion (with drawings and other representations as stimuli).

> The important thing, from the point of view of libertarian education, is for men to come to feel like masters of their thinking by discussing the thinking and views of the world explicitly or implicitly manifest in their own suggestions and those of their comrades. Because this view of education starts with the conviction that it cannot present its own program but must search for this program dialogically with the people, it serves to introduce the pedagogy of the oppressed, in the elaboration of which the oppressed must participate. (Freire, 1970, p. 118)

In countries where literacy levels are relatively high in the population, the teaching of literacy to adults is a different matter and one that has been recognised as a challenge only fairly late in the twentieth century. Street (1995) has described the development of adult literacy teaching in the UK which, he suggests, was the first industrialised society to recognise its necessity in the 1970s. There was a national BBC TV campaign in which a series of programmes raised awareness and guided potential students to local provision. That local provision was based on volunteer tutors, teaching adults one-to-one. The teaching methods varied with the tutors, who received little or no training but they tended to be individual, learner-centred, and frequently based on material the students themselves wished to read or write. Freirean methods were part of the teaching discourse at the time if not so often part of the teaching practice. Following this initial phase, Street describes a second one in the 1980s in which there was a shift from volunteer and one-to-one teaching towards classes taught by tutors employed in designated centres. There was funding pressure to move away from learner-centred methods to workforce skills preparation under the umbrella of 'adult basic education'. There was increasing emphasis by central government and its principal agency in the field, the Adult Literacy and Basic Skills Unit, with assessing student learning against explicit general criteria. In the third (current) phase distinguished by Street these trends have been accentuated by centralised funding arrangements and a system of national vocational qualifications. The resulting teaching to specific attainment targets, whatever its merits, is a long way from the learner-centred approaches which characterised methods years ago. Literacy teaching with adults, as with children, is in state of constant flux. There are similar tensions in the two fields in reconciling the need to respond to individual learners and the need to attain objectives although, given the characteristics of adult learners, it is unlikely that it will ever be practicable for objectives-led teaching to be taken as far in adult literacy teaching.

Making Sense of Different Methods

We have reached the end of this chapter without having reviewed all aspects of all methods of teaching literacy. There has not been space, for example, to consider methods of integrating the teaching of writing with the teaching of reading, methods for extending literacy after the initial phase of teaching, methods for the many children nowadays who are learning literacy in an additional language, or methods for learners who experience difficulties. To cover all these would take a book or several books. This chapter, however, has not been so much about methods themselves as about *reflecting* on methods. I have attempted, first, to argue that it is worth being reflective about methods and, second, to provide some ways of doing that in terms of identifying assumptions made within methods about paradigmatic teaching situations, the nature of teaching and learning, and the prioritisation of literacy levels. All teaching methods – past, present and future – can be examined in these terms. They need to be if we are to avoid the 'absolutism and one-sided dogmatism' referred to at the beginning of the chapter.

Further Reading

There is a vast and continually expanding literature on methods of teaching literacy. The following go into detail which it has not been possible to cover in this chapter and they are jumping off points for further study.

ADAMS, M.J. (1990) *Beginning to Read: Thinking and Learning about Print*, Cambridge, MA: MIT Press. Marilyn Jager Adams was commissioned by the Center for the Study at the University of Illinois to produce a review of research into phonics and reading teaching. This 420 page report was the result. It is a lucid account of a complex research literature and therefore an excellent starting point for studying this aspect of teaching methods. An eight–page 'afterword' by two members of the Center's advisory panel for the review, Dorothy Strickland and Bernice Cullinan, regretted that Adams did not place phonics within a broader framework of language learning but praised the style and scholarship of her review.

BEARD, R. (1990) *Developing Reading 3–13* (2nd edn), London: Hodder and Stoughton.

BEARD, R. (Ed) (1993) *Teaching Literacy, Balancing Perspectives*, London: Hodder and Stoughton. These two books provide a useful account of methods of literacy teaching, particularly in relation to the UK. Beard has his own views on key issues but they are presented explicitly enough to be examined alongside others described.

DEPARTMENT FOR EDUCATION AND EMPLOYMENT (1998) *The National Literacy Strategy: Framework for Teaching*, London: DfEE. The National Literacy Strategy is changing methods of teaching in England. Although the *Framework* is more concerned with what should be taught than how it should be taught there is a description in this document of the 'literacy hour' and an account of what is now expected by the government in relation, for example, to group teaching methods.

HANNON, P. (1995) *Literacy, Home and School: Research and Practice in Teaching Literacy with Parents*, London: Falmer Press. Provides an overview of theory and methods and research in involving parents in the teaching of literacy.

NEUMAN, S.B., and ROSKOS, K.A. (Eds) (1998) *Children Achieving: Best Practices in Early Literacy*, Newark, DE: International Reading Association. This book collects accounts from several contributors who write about a range of methods for the inital teaching of literacy, mainly in relation to the North American context. The collection as a whole reflects a less 'instructional' approach than is now being established in England and as such is an interesting contrast to the DfEE *Framework for Teaching*.

PRESSLEY, M. (1998) *Reading Instruction that Works: The Case for Balanced Teaching*, New York: Guilford Press. Michael Pressley, writing in a US context, provided in this book a clear and extensive research-based overview of methods of literacy teaching including those needed beyond the initial phase.

Chapter 6

Researching Literacy in Education

Overview

Previous chapters have drawn on a wide range of research studies. One way to reflect on literacy in education is to carry out research into it or to engage with other people's research. The framing of research questions, as well as the findings which result from trying to answer them, can clarify our ideas. Research can reveal the nature of literacy in a range of contexts. Even when it cannot tell what *is* the case in a specific context, it can open our minds to what *may be* the case.

The aim of this chapter is to introduce some key ideas about educational research as it is conducted in relation to literacy – particularly at Master's level. Many readers of this book will carry out some research themselves into topics such as teaching methods, literacy development, the nature of past, present and future literacy, and its social and political significance. The focus here is on empirical research, that is research which involves the collection of data. Other kinds of research are important, including historical/archival, philosophical, textual, theoretical research and the critical synthesising and reviewing of previous research but they will not be covered here. The dividing line between empirical and non-empirical research is not absolute but, broadly, empirical research can be regarded as research which could not be carried out within a library but which requires us to go out and discover something in the world.

The aim is not to repeat all the information readily available in educational research guides (some of which are listed in the further reading at the end of the chapter) but to show that there are many methods which have been used to understand literacy in education and which deserve to be considered by new researchers in the field. The chapter considers the nature of data in literacy research and whether it can be quantified. Four research designs – case studies, surveys, longitudinal studies and experiments – are briefly reviewed. Evaluation is considered as a specific kind of research. The aim is to reflect on the strengths and weaknesses of various kinds of research so that readers may have a better critical appreciation of other people's research and be better prepared to plan their own research. First, however, it is necessary to reflect on what is distinctive about literacy research.

Literacy as a Field of Research

Literacy is a *multidisciplinary* field of research. Already in this book we have encountered research studies from the disciplines of psychology, sociology, linguistics, anthropology, politics, history, and curriculum studies. This is one reason why literacy is such a fascinating topic. It challenges our understanding and our theories at every level of explanation and investigation. It is also a reason why researching literacy is difficult. It is hard to use several disciplines simultaneously but if we stay within the confines of just one there is a danger of reaching conclusions that cannot withstand scrutiny from another disciplinary perspective. For example, it can be misleading to study family literacy programmes solely in terms of psychological processes while ignoring social aspects or to explore emancipation and empowerment through literacy without considering curricular realities.

In the past, psychological approaches were dominant in educational research into literacy and many problems continue to be framed in purely psychological terms (e.g. 'reading ability'). However, over the years – particularly during the 1990s – other disciplines have converged on literacy. David Barton (1994) characterises the changes in this way:

> At different points in history disciplines go forward at different rates; in the past decade the pace of change in the study of reading and writing has been rapid and the new field of literacy studies has come into existence. It is important to realize that there is a significant paradigm shift going on in this area. It is exhibited in various ways, one of the most visible being the explosion of books, papers and conferences on the subject. The shift is in a particular direction. Many of the recent works I will refer to begin with summaries of changes in views and they all are shifts to some social perspective. (Barton, 1994, p. 6)

We could even cite the appearance of this book in a series for Masters' students as an illustration of what is happening. Not many years ago it would have seemed rather odd to have a book on literacy in education; now it seems to be a core topic, of great interest to many practitioners and researchers.

When a new field of research, at the intersection of several disciplines, emerges it is natural that it is also a site for controversy, debate and struggle over definitions of terms and theoretical models. Hence Barton devotes two chapters of his book just to defining terms and establishing what 'literacy' refers to. The consequences for new researchers entering the field is that they have to be very aware that terms they use may not be well understood by others unless they are carefully defined and the methods and theories they use may be rejected unless they are carefully justified.

Literacy Data

It is well known that 'data' are what researchers collect and analyse but what kinds of data are there in literacy research? The origin of the word 'data' is the plural of the Latin word 'datum' meaning 'that which is given'. It entered the vocabulary of researchers at a time in the past when it seemed to many of them that the task of research was to collect facts in the world and then make sense of them. Now it is clearer that data are not so much given as constructed. What counts as data depends on the concepts and interests researchers bring to a situation. This is not to say that data can be constructed out of thin air but it does mean that we have to look critically at the concepts and assumptions underlying data collection.

Texts – pieces of writing – are perhaps the obvious form of data in literacy research whether they are studied as what people read or what they read. Analysing young children's writing can reveal its development and processes such as invented spelling. The writing of researchers can reveal how they seek to communicate and promote their research within the research community. Textual study is important for studying reading development too, e.g. the preferences of boys and girls for different kinds of books.

It is seldom possible, however, to answer research questions solely by reference to the texts. Literacy is not only written language but also the uses of written language and to understand those we need to know how and why texts are produced or read. Some kind of *observation* is needed to understand the conditions of the use of texts – how they fit into social practices. An account of children's writing, for example, is incomplete if we do not know what moved them to write, who they thought their audience was, whether they were asked to produce something, what instructions they were given, whether the writing was spontaneous, and so on.

Different depths of observation are possible. At a basic level, it can simply be watching and recording contexts and action as an observer, say, sitting at the back of a classroom. At a deeper level, it might involve trying to understand how participants experience a social situation – what it means to them. In *ethnography* researchers attempt to do this by immersing themselves in the lives of participants over a length of time and regularly writing up their observations, reflections and hypotheses. The data here are the ethnographer's notes.

A common way of trying to find out what people do or think is to ask them. *Interviewing* is the staple method of educational research. It can either be structured so that all informants are asked a carefully prepared set of questions in a fixed order or semi-structured in which there is more flexibility or unstructured in which the researcher's questions arise out of dialogue with participants.

Questionnaires can be regarded as a way of conducting a structured interview through written, rather than oral, language – without the researcher being present. Informants are given questions in writing and asked to respond in writing or by marking pre-set answers. The advantage of questionnaires is that they can save the researcher time and effort, thus permitting data collection from more informants – but the disadvantages are that the researchers is not available to clarify or adjust questions and, perhaps for that reason, questionnaires often have very low response rates.

Finally, there are *tasks, assessments and tests*. These cover a wide variety of ways in which researchers have sought to investigate and measure literacy skills.

They include reacting to words or non-words flashed on a screen, spelling tests in which children write from dictation, oral or silent reading tests. Common to them all is a degree of artificiality, that is they are contrived for research purposes and do not form part of any social practice (other than 'being assessed' or 'participating in an experiment'). This always raises problems of validity but contrived tasks do yield data useful for both theoretical and evaluative research.

Quantitative or Non-quantitative Methods?

An issue which has troubled many researchers and practitioners is how far one can go in quantifying literacy data. If data can be expressed in terms of numbers it becomes possible to carry out statistical analyses of differences and relationships but it could be argued that literacy is beyond quantification, that it belongs to the realm of meaning, social relationships and language where the important things are beyond measurement. To assess the seriousness of such objections we need to look at the nature of quantification and quantitative data analysis.

Quantitative methods is that they are often juxtaposed with 'qualitative' methods as if these were opposites. This discourse is not helpful. All researchers are concerned with qualitative issues – with trying to understand the qualities of things. It is preferable to talk of *quantitative* and *non-quantitative* methods. I, for example, am a researcher who sometimes uses quantitative methods, and sometimes does not, and I am unwilling to accept the implication that when I turn to quantitative methods, I am no longer concerned with qualities. Therefore in what follows I will not use the word 'qualitative' when what is really meant is 'non-quantitative'.

There have been advocates of either quantitative or non-quantitative methods who have asserted the superiority of their preferred approach. Here is an example of how quantitative methods have been advocated and non-quantitative methods implicitly denigrated:

> To 'know' a person really means to be able to describe him [*sic*] accurately and fully . . . We may be content to describe him roughly and qualitatively, or we may try to describe him more precisely and in quantitative terms. The more we try to make our description precise and quantitative, the more we get involved in measurement. (Thorndike and Hagen, 1969, pp. 8–9)

Here is how some advocates of non-quantitative methods have criticised quantitative methods in evaluation research.

> Students – rather like plant crops – are given pre-tests (the seedlings are weighed or measured) and then submitted to different experiences (treatment conditions). Subsequently, after a period of time, their attainment (growth or yield) is measured to indicate the relative efficiency of the methods (fertilisers) used. Studies of this kind are designed to yield data of one particular type, i.e. 'objective' numerical data that permit statistical analyses. (Parlett and Hamilton, 1977, pp. 7–8)

These quotations, in the disparaging characterisation of the criticised approach, and in the indirectness of the methodological critique, are typical of debates in this area but we need to consider the issue more deeply.

What lies behind the mistrust of quantitative methods? There would appear to be no convincing epistemological reason for thinking that they represent an *inherently false* way of understanding educational phenomena. It must be admitted that quantification has sometimes been oversold. There is the view of Thorndike and Hagen (1969), quoted above, which suggested that non-quantitative descriptions of people can only be 'rough' whereas quantitative descriptions are 'precise' (one wonders what novelists they ever read). This echoes nineteenth-century views that science depended upon measurement. A more telling objection to quantification is that it encourages the reification of concepts. A clear example of this in educational psychology would be the concept of IQ as an individual's fixed intellectual potential when it is really no more than a statistical expression of how an individual's performance on a restricted range of tasks compares to others of the same age in the population. Quantification can be a cloak for intellectual superficiality – one does read research reports where a mass of quantitative data obscures weak conceptualisation of a research issue. Quantification can be particularly problematic in evaluation studies where the outcome measures used may not be valid indicators of a programme's aims. It should be noted, however, that all these difficulties with quantitative methods – being oversold, being associated with reification and invalidity also occur with non-quantitative methods.

Perhaps part of the unease with quantification is due to anxieties about the use of mathematics – specifically statistics. Maths anxiety is widespread in the population even among the academically successful who become educational researchers (who knows – it might even be more common in those who opt for studies in language and literacy). The rejection of quantification may be based on misunderstandings about what it means. Just as there are many non-quantitative methods there is a wide range of quantitative possibilities. It should be noted in passing that there are many other ways in which research approaches differ (e.g. in terms of the purpose of the research, whether the aim is to generalise, how research questions are formulated, sampling, what kinds of data are used and how the research is reported and shared with others) which may be more crucial for understanding and judging them than whether or not quantitative methods are used.

Quantification is an entirely 'natural' way of understanding the world. Some of the earliest examples of writing (Sumerian cuneiform clay tablets and many prehistoric 'tallies') relate to counting objects, events or time. Counting is one level of quantification which merges into another level, measuring. It is worth distinguishing four levels altogether. The 'categorial' (or 'nominal') level is where numbers refer to counts of how many items are in a particular category, (e.g. how many adults believe they have literacy difficulties, how many are men or women, how many teachers have ever undertaken Masters' courses). Sometimes it can be difficult to define the boundaries of a category (e.g. defining a teacher of literacy) but once a categorisation has been made one can count the number in a category. In an 'ordinal' (or 'ranked') level of quantification the numbers indicate something different – the relative positions in an order, e.g. English SAT (standard assessment task) scores, social class, degree level, essay/exam grades. The 'interval' level of measurement is similar to the ordinal except that the distances between numbers are assumed to be equal or are constructed to be so, e.g. reading age, standardised reading test score. The fourth level of quantification, the 'ratio' level, is an interval scale where '0' means absolute zero, and '4', say, is twice '2', e.g. age in months, time taken to recognise words. These four levels differ in terms of the assumptions about the data and in terms of the statistical procedures which can be validly used to analyse the data. In educational research, some of these levels of quantification may be more problematic than others. For example, categorial quantification generally requires fewer assumptions (or suspensions of belief) than interval level measurement. Objections which can be held with respect to one level may not be relevant to another.

It is also helpful to recognise that there are at least three kinds of analyses which can be undertaken in relation to any kind of quantitative data.

1   Descriptive: simply describing a dataset (e.g. how many cases in different categories, the mean scores or spread of test scores in a sample)
2   Comparative: exploring differences between sub-groups (e.g. differences in percentages of different cases, differences in mean scores or the spread of scores)
3   Relational/inferential: concerning the relationships between variables (e.g. correlation, regression)

When we reflect on the fact that any of these different kinds of analyses might be carried out with data quantified at any one of the four levels described earlier we can see that there are many possibilities to be considered. *Figure 3* represents the possibilities as cells in a matrix.

There are twelve cells in this matrix. The upper left cell represents kinds of data analyses which are very different from those in lower right in terms of the methodological assumptions to be made about data and in terms of the complexity of the statistical analyses which might be used. If the possibilities are 'unpacked' in this way it becomes clear how unwise it is to lump all of them together in either blanket condemnation or blanket approval of quantitative methods. In judging the appropriateness of quantitative methods, it is important to be clear which variety one is talking about.

Some Masters' students find it difficult to decide whether to use quantitative methods in their research studies. It is to be hoped that they allow themselves a *genuine* choice. This depends not only on being aware of the possibilities of quantification but also on being aware of the quantitative aspects of their particular topic. Almost all empirical studies have quantitative aspects – if one fails to recognise them it is hard to see how one can judge whether or not they are worth pursuing. In any research judgements have to be made about the costs and bene-

Figure 3: Twelve kinds of data analysis

	Descriptive	Comparative	Relational
Categorial			
Ordinal			
Interval			
Ratio			

fits of different approaches. The costs of using quantitative approaches might include learning to use statistical software which – especially on the first occasion – may take up valuable time. Against this there may be benefits in terms of clearer findings and the student's own professional development. Assuming that the researcher does have a genuine choice about which methods to use what then matters is being clear about the research aims of the study or the research questions to be addressed. No method or technique can compensate for confusion over aims. Aims may dictate a non-quantitative or quantitative approach. Ultimately what matters is that methods fit purposes.

There is a paramount need to be critical in carrying out one's own research and in engaging with other people's research. In the case of quantitative methodology, the Radical Statistics Education Group (1982) proposed some key questions for critically reviewing research carried out and published by others: Do measures appropriately represent underlying concepts (construct validity)? Would there have been different results with different samples (sampling error)? Could tenable alternative hypotheses account for results (e.g. 'third variables')? Can the results be generalised (external validity)? Was the analysis conducted at the right level (e.g. classes/individuals)? Are the statistical procedures explained? Are the conclusions wider than the results warrant? Is there any evidence of fabrication of data or deception? In designing one's own study it is helpful to reflect on how one would answer these questions if challenged. In this way one can develop a more critical appreciation of the use of quantitative methods.

> It is socially acceptable to be baffled and bemused by numbers. This is a regrettable state of affairs and means that large sections of the population feel unable to challenge decisions made on the basis of expert technical advice. We hope that people with no more than basic numerical skills – and we would regard the possession of

these as a reasonable and important goal for everyone – will be able to apply our ideas when the results from the next educational research project hits the headlines: 'NEW RESEARCH SHOWS' . . . Does it? (Radical Statistics Education Group, 1982)

Four Basic Research Designs

Empirical research into literacy in education is not just a matter of collecting data or of analysing it. It also involves some overall plan or *design* which gives the data collection and analysis some purpose and coherence. There are four designs worth mentioning here – case studies, surveys, longitudinal studies and experimental studies.

Case studies are an approach to understanding through detailed investigation of one or a few instances of some topic of interest. In *surveys* many cases are studied – necessarily less intensively than in case studies but still in a systematic way. *Longitudinal studies* are a special form of case study or survey in which cases are studied over a sufficiently long period of time for age-related changes in cases to be investigated or for the effects of curriculum to be detected. Finally, in *experimental studies* researchers seek to manipulate key variables in order to investigate causal relationships more directly than is possible in other research designs. Each of these designs has strengths and weaknesses which make them a good choice for tackling some research questions but less good for others.

Case studies

If one is interested in a topic in literacy in education the most obvious research approach is to study an example – a case – of it. The 'case' could be an adult learning to write, a child reading for information, the implementation of a family literacy project, a literacy tutor's life history, a reading scheme or a college department – almost anything in fact. A 'case' does not have to be an individual person. It might, for example, be a class of thirty individuals or it could be an entire nation composed of millions of citizens. There can be 'cases', too, where no persons are studied directly, e.g. software programs, print environments, text structure. All that matters is that the case is an example of the category of things which are of interest or that it exhibits such features that studying it is bound to be illuminating.

Case studies can make use of a wide range of research methods – interviews, participant observations, non-participant observation. They can involve experimental methods and statistical analyses (Neuman and McCormick, 1995). However, there has been a tendency since the late 1970s to associate the case study approach with non-quantitative methods. This may be because studying just one case (or a handful of cases) gives researchers the opportunity to delve more deeply and to use detailed descriptive methods including ethnography.

One problem with case studies is that they are by definition particular whereas in research we are often interested in the general. How can we be sure that finding out about a particular case will tell us anything of interest beyond that case? This is the vexed problem of generalisation in the social sciences – a problem by no means confined to case study methods. Here we need to be clear about the aims of research studies and the kinds of generalisation which are sought. Sometimes the aim is to produce true generalisations of the kind, 'All reading requires a given level of phonemic awareness' or 'Increased literacy rates are the result, not the cause, of economic growth in societies'. But there are different kinds of truth which research can reveal, and research aims are often more modest. A case study may enlarge our appreciation of what may be occurring in other situations rather than what is occurring. For example, Heath's (1983) study of communities in the southern states of the US does not tell us directly what is happening in, say, inner city Sheffield, but it may give us a wider appreciation of what could be happening so encouraging us to think twice about our assumptions concerning family literacy in particular communities or to ask fresh research questions. Also, it can sometimes be worth studying a unique case even where there is no current possibility of generalising to similar cases, e.g. a classroom where each child has a personal computer. The aim then might be theoretical generalisation rather than empirical generalisation.

Often, in case study research more than one case will be studied. There could be parallel case studies of, say, the literacy activities of several workers in one organisation or of special needs provision in several local education authorities. It can be illuminating to choose contrasting cases (e.g. family literacy in middle class and working class homes, literacy curricula in different countries). However, the essence of case study is that cases can be studied in a relatively detailed way.

Surveys

If the number of cases in a study increases, resources (particularly researchers' time) have to be spread more thinly and the opportunity for detailed study is reduced. At some point it makes more sense to refer to the study as a *survey* of a number of cases. There are no hard and fast rules about how many cases it takes to make a survey but it would be unusual to have a case study with cases numbered in double figures or a survey with the number of cases in single figures.

It is hardly necessary to explain to readers of this book what surveys are since they have become so much a part of everyday life in Western industrialised societies. It is difficult to open a newspaper or tune into radio or TV news without hearing about the results of some survey or other. Many people will also have had the experience of participating in a survey, e.g. at work, as a consumer, or in a national census.

Surveys involve the systematic collection of information about a large number of cases (often more than any one person would ordinarily encounter). There is an attempt to reduce bias by producing findings which relate to all cases in a target population. Surveys, like other forms of research, have a political dimension. There is usually a definite purpose for collecting certain information. Researchers do not just stumble across 'social facts' – a survey is one way of creating such 'facts'.

Surveys are often thought of in terms of interviewing a sample of people (using a standard set of questions in an *interview schedule*) or distributing question-naires. However, the cases in a survey can be just as varied as cases in case study, i.e. they can be people, organisations, countries, places, things, activities, literacy practices, and so on. Also the methods used to study the various cases need not be confined to interviews and questionnaires. One could have direct or indirect observation, or documentary analysis. Even when interviews or questionnaires are used, these can be closed or open-ended, undertaken in person or via tele-phone or email.

There are some semi-technical terms which can help in talking about and plan-ning surveys. First there is the *target population* – the people, places or things about which we want to know more. The survey is, as it were, aimed at the target population. However, for practical reasons, some of the target population may be beyond the reach of the survey (e.g. students may be absent from class on the day when they are to complete a questionnaire). Therefore in practice the *survey pop-ulation* may be smaller than the target population. Obviously, the less it differs from the target population, the better. Even when the survey population has been adequately defined it may not be necessary or possible to survey every case because of lack of time, researchers or other resources. A *sample* of cases is selected. Here it is important to select sufficient cases to enable generalisations to the survey population.

One should strive for an unbiased selection – something which can often be achieved by some form of *random sampling*. This is an important consideration even in small scale research. With a little thought it is usually possible to find some way of choosing cases at random (e.g. by taking every sixth name on a reg-ister, using random number tables, or even by picking names out of a hat). Some-times sampling is carried out in stages, e.g. identifying key groups and then sampling at random from each group ('stratified random sampling') or sampling from a previously drawn sample. Finally, it often happens that information is not obtained for all those surveyed (e.g. respondents may not return their question-naires). The *response rate* (the percentage of the sample surveyed for which infor-mation was obtained) needs to be reasonably high if the results of a survey are to have validity. This can be difficult to obtain with some kinds of surveys (e.g. postal questionnaire surveys may achieve only a 50–60 per cent response rate even with well-planned follow-up prompts) although other kinds can be much more successful (e.g. personal interviewing by teachers of parents in their homes may achieve close to a 100 per cent response rate).

Some basic principles apply to the analysis of survey data whether one is analysing hundreds or thousands of cases using computer software or just a few cases by hand. The essence of a survey is that the same information (e.g. respon-dents' replies to specific questions) is collected about a set of cases and that some kind of summary is produced. The first step is usually to collate all the bits of information relating to each point across all cases (e.g. how everyone answered question number 8), if necessary *coding* replies into a manageable set of cate-gories or producing some descriptive statistics. When this has been done for all variables it is usually possible to produce an overall description of the survey sample. The next stage is to look at *relationships* between variables (e.g. one might be interested in how reading test scores relate to the sex of pupils).

Longitudinal studies

Longitudinal studies are single cases or samples studied over a long period of time. They are difficult to undertake but the data they yield can be enormously valuable. In literacy there have been longitudinal case studies of single children (sometimes undertaken by the child's parent or grandparent) and some large studies which have collected literacy data among other measures.

Experimental studies

Surveys and longitudinal studies can reveal associations or correlations between variables where we suspect that there is a causal relationship, e.g. that preschool parent involvement fosters literacy development. Causation is difficult – if not impossible – to establish in descriptive studies. Instead one needs an experimental study in which a supposed causative factor can be varied and its effects observed. In a 'true experimental design' a sample of cases (often individual children or learners but possibly larger units such as classes or schools) is divided strictly at random between an experimental group (or several such groups) and a control group. The experimental group is then treated in a different way – receiving some kind of programme or experience which the control group does not. Afterwards data are collected from both groups to see if there have been any effects (on the 'dependent variable'). The idea of an experiment, like that of an interview or survey, is basically simple and widely understood. In practice, however, the simplicity is often compromised by not having random allocation to groups. Allocation on any other basis introduces other factors which makes interpretation of differences between the two groups uncertain. Another difficulty with experiments is that one has to be careful that the 'treatment' of the experimental group does involve changing the factor being studied and that the data collected on both treatment and outcomes are valid.

Evaluation

There is increasing interest and activity in exploring new ways of promoting literacy learning in and out of school. Some literacy initiatives take place within particular communities, areas, schools or organisations. Others are national or are of clear national significance. Large scale initiatives often have smaller ones nested within them. All need to be evaluated to some degree.

Evaluation is a form of research in which any of the methods and issues already discussed can be relevant but it is helpful also to note that evaluation tends to differ from other kinds of research in at least two respects. First, the research questions to be answered in evaluation are determined by practical demands – the need to know the value of a course of action and whether it achieves its purposes. Other kinds of research are driven more by curiosity, the need to understand, and the demands of theory building. Second, evaluation is usually more resource constrained than other kinds of research. Practical demands mean that an answer has to be provided by a certain time within a fixed budget. Other kinds of research can be more easily prolonged until answers are found. For individuals working with limited time and resources it is obviously not reasonable to attempt to produce conclusive, documented 'proof' that what is done in a literacy initiative is successful. It might be enough to document what has been done and to collect participants' views about its value. However, a well-funded project of national significance, involving many learners and practitioners, has an obligation to do much more.

Why evaluate? If we try something new in literacy education we ought to evaluate it. Without evaluation of some kind we cannot be sure that we are accomplishing what we set out to do, and we cannot show other people (who may make funding decisions) that what we are doing is valuable. Without evaluation we are at the mercy of educational fashion and prejudice.

It is important to recognise that – as the term suggests – 'evaluation' is about values. Many values in literacy education are widely held. Most people, for example, want children to be competent readers, good spellers, to enjoy books, and so on; and parents to be confident about their own capacities as teachers and learners. But problems arise when values conflict, or we want to give priority to one over another. For example, is it more important that children are excited by writing and want to communicate or that they spell accurately? Here the process of evaluation ought to involve making our values and priorities clear. The evaluation ought to reflect the values in our practice. There is no point, for example, in evaluating a programme by testing children's reading accuracy on standardised measures if what we really value is children's enjoyment of shared stories.

Another important point about evaluation is that it is about choosing between options. At the very least the options are to run a programme or to leave things as they are. If we are in a situation of genuinely having no options, it is probably a waste of effort to conduct an evaluation. Where there are options an evaluation ought to try to compare what was done to some reasonable alternative. What else might literacy learners have experienced? Would it have been any better? How else might we have spent our energies?

Writing is an essential part of evaluation. Even if time is short and the evaluator is the only person likely to read an evaluation, it is still worth writing something – perhaps only a paragraph or two. The very act of writing about what we have done helps us to concentrate on it, distances us from the immediacy of action, and enables us to reflect and learn from experience. Writing also opens up the possibility of sharing our experience with others. Research and evaluation is a way of telling a story of what happened in a literacy initiative in terms which can enable others to judge its relevance and value for their situation. It should also tell that story in a systematic and inquiring manner. The structure, length and content of an evaluation report can be envisaged at the start of an initiative so that, from the very beginning, the evaluation activity and the writing can be linked.

Description of context

The first step in evaluating a literacy initiative should be to describe the setting in which it takes place. It is impossible to reach a view about the value of some action without relating it to a particular context. Writing this down helps us identify assumptions underlying our practice and enables other people to work out the relevance of our experience for their situation.

Clearly stated aims

Undertaking an evaluation requires clearly stated aims for an initiative. What are the desired *outcomes*? The first objective ought then to be to find out how far the stated aims have been met. There may be scope for finding out about other things too but that should not be at the expense of the central task.

Building on previous research

It is hard to imagine any literacy initiative which is so innovative that it cannot be related to other people's work and to previously reported evaluations. We should not waste time reinventing the wheel. Also, readers of a report will want to know what this evaluation adds to what is already known in a field. Therefore some part of the evaluation effort ought to go into finding out and summarising previous work.

More than tests

It is often assumed that evaluation of literacy programmes should be based on tests but this can sometimes be inappropriate. There are some worthwhile alternatives to be considered first. A preliminary question which an evaluation ought to address concerns *take-up*. How many of those invited to participate in programme actually take up the invitation? If the proportion is very low, that suggests at once that the programme may have limited value. If it is high, we can go on to ask further questions. Those who participate in an initiative may not stay with it. Hence it is important to monitor *participation* and *drop-out*. (*Stop-out* – leaving and then returning to a programme – is important too). It takes thought and record-keeping to document this but the effort is worthwhile for we can learn something about the value of an initiative from how people 'vote with their feet'. The *implementation* of an initiative is crucial. How it works in practice can be significantly different from what was planned. Information about what was done, what it actually cost, the knock-on effects, and so on can be very helpful in reaching a view about the value of an initiative. An evaluation can explore the *quality of processes in an initiative and associated programmes*. This can be a challenge. Every initiative has processes of some kind. These can occur, for example, in the provision of adult education, in parent-child talk about environmental print, in conversation in a parents' group, or in a teacher professional development course. It is often worth reflecting on the quality of what goes on. One does not have to be very sophisticated to reach conclusions. For example, if, in a parent group, only one or two ever contribute to the discussion or, in classroom writing, pupils are restricted to a single genre, there are grounds for questioning whether the process is as valuable as was hoped.

Literacy initiatives are more than abstract ideas, plans or documents. They are about people doing things together. The participants can include parents, other family members, teachers, and other professionals as well as children. Therefore it makes sense to seek *participants' views*. The conventional ways of doing this are through interviews, questionnaires, noting conversations. Much depends on the resources (time, money) available for the evaluation but, even when time and money are short, some way can usually be found to check on participants' views.

Outcomes

The main question which an evaluation ought to answer is whether or not the initiative has secured the desired outcomes. This takes us back to the aims. Note that the outcomes could be activities (e.g. frequency of library use) as well as changes in literacy development (e.g. better writing).

Using tests to evaluate initiatives

Is there a case for using tests to measure outcomes in literacy development? The answer is 'yes' but only if one is satisfied on three counts. First, tests are not a substitute for the other components of evaluation already discussed. Second, tests need to be valid and to reflect the initiative aims. It can be difficult to find tests which meet these criteria, especially for adults and for young children. Third, the test scores of learners in an initiative have to be compared to something – on their own they are meaningless. There are many possible comparisons – to pre-programme scores, to national norms, to a control group – but each has pitfalls. One should be very confident that the pitfalls are known, and can be avoided, before allowing a literacy initiative to be judged on the basis of test data. Evaluation issues relating to the use of tests, and alternative approaches, are discussed in more detail in Hannon (1995).

Time and resources for evaluation

As a general principle I suggest that, in a new initiative, around 10 per cent of staff time (and other funds) should be allowed for evaluation. A particularly innovative initiative, of wide interest, might deserve more than 10 per cent – perhaps as much as 50 per cent or more. A more routine programme might require

Figure 4: The evaluation checklist

Points to consider in an evaluation

   1 Description of context

   2 Clarification of aims and desired outcomes

   3 Previous research

   4 Programme/initiatitive description

   5 Take up

   6 Participation, stop-out and drop-out

   7 Implementation

   8 Quality of processes

   9 Participants' views

10 Outcomes in activities

11 Outcomes in literacy measures

---

5 per cent or less. Allowing a certain proportion of resources in this way is not self-indulgent; in the end it is about the quality of what is offered. If the 5 per cent or 10 per cent only amounts to a few hours of one person's time, the evaluation is probably going to consist of keeping records and notes during the initiative, and sitting down quietly at the end to reflect in writing on what has happened. If it amounts to several days of time, then one is in a position to share what has been learned with others who might want to do the same.

Figure 4 is a checklist which summarises key points about evaluation.

Choosing and Planning a Research Study

Some readers of this book will go on to choose a literacy topic for their research – typically for a dissertation. Some know what they want to do for their dissertations even before they start a course. Others decide at a very late stage. In my experience the two approaches are equally likely to result in a good dissertation (or a bad one) but there is nothing wrong in taking time to choose a topic. Jumping at the first idea to come along, and getting over-committed to it too soon, can lead to difficulties later.

Choosing a topic is made easier if one allows a little time for the choosing process. Reading around areas of interest, talking to friends, fellow students and tutors about possibilities (and talking about what one does *not* want to do) and writing can help considerably at this stage. Free writing techniques (a few minutes writing whatever comes into your mind) can open up possibilities, particularly if it is connected prose about one's ideas.

It often helps to have more than one idea. Having options means more control over – and therefore more confidence in – what one eventually decides to study. Listing options can create new ones. Merging options is another way to shape a research topic.

One very important aspect of developing a research topic is to *identify one or more research questions*. I have yet to come across a research topic, at dissertation or any other level, which cannot be usefully clarified in terms of questions. Questions help one identify what one really wants to achieve in a research study. A question written down can be shared with others and examined critically. We can ask, is this actually a *researchable* question (sadly, some interesting questions are not researchable).

As soon as one has decided on a research topic and the associated research questions, one is in a position to plan a dissertation study. To a large extent a research study, including the planning of it, is a *writing task*. Therefore it is worth thinking about what has to be written and when. More will be said about this in the next chapter. At an early stage it is worth producing an outline for the dissertation, with chapter headings, an indication of the content of chapters, and roughly how many words to be allowed for each. The dissertation outline will, of course, change as the study develops but it is always valuable for the student and supervisor to have a map of where the study is going and how far there is to go. This can prevent unnecessary detours. It is worth trying to write *something*, however little, each week. Little bits mount up, and, even if one revises drafts later, writing up at the end of your study will be much easier by writing as one goes along.

There are other things to plan in a research study and it is worth giving time to producing a good plan at the outset. At some point all, or some, of the following will have to be done.

> Identify one's basic interests
> Review the relevant research literature
> Formulate researchable questions or aims
> Choose appropriate research methods
> Possibly try out methods in a pilot study and revise them if necessary.
> Collect data or material
> Analyse data or material
> Identify points for discussion and implications arising from the study
> Identify key conclusion

A literature review of previous research is essential for your dissertation (typically it takes up one or two chapters, 5,000 words or so). More will be said about this too in the next chapter. One may have certain 'leads' on previous research (e.g. from a course unit or an assignment you have done) but a systematic search is still necessary.

One needs to decide on the appropriate methods for answering research questions. The early part of this chapter should help. Even if one chooses not to use certain methods it is necessary to explain in a dissertation why obvious possibilities were rejected, especially if they are used by other researchers. Whatever the methods, it is often possible to try them out on a small scale before getting completely committed. A pilot study can iron out difficulties and make life easier in the main study.

Collecting data – whether from people or by examining documents – takes time, and the researcher is often not in control of when and where data is to be collected. For example, colleges or schools may be closed or busy just at the time when the researcher is free to conduct interviews with staff; survey respondents may not return questionnaires by a deadline; a teacher can be off sick just in the period planned for classroom observation. A well-planned timetable, with margins for slippage, will minimise the problems. The study plan should indicate the planned beginning and end of data collection.

Data analysis is a further stage in a study for which a researcher needs some advance idea of what he or she will do and for which time needs to be budgeted. The details here are something to be sorted out in collaboration with a supervisor.

The final stage in a study is about understanding its significance. It can sometimes be hard to see the wood for the trees by the end. What have I really discovered? Is it what I originally set out to find or have I redefined the problem? It often helps to go back to the previous research literature at this stage and ask, 'What have I added (in however small a way) to what was known before?' The answers to these questions govern what is written about in the Discussions/Implications/Conclusions chapters/sections of your dissertation.

An awareness of these stages of a small scale study such as a dissertation can help generate an effective plan and timetable. However, one should always keep *Hofstadter's Law* in mind. Hofstadter's Law states that, 'Everything takes longer than you expect it to – even after you have allowed for Hofstadter's Law'.

Further Reading

I am not aware of any book devoted to methods of researching literacy in education and those on general methods of educational research all have their limitations. Nevertheless, the following may be useful.

BELL, J. (1993) *Doing your Research Project: A Guide for First-Time Researchers in Education and the Social Sciences*, Buckingham: Open University Press. This book complements the one by Cohen and Manion in that it discusses practical issues which precede and follow using particular methods.

COHEN, L. and MANION, L. (1994) *Research Methods in Education (4th edn)*, London: Routledge. Cohen and Manion attempt to provide an introduction to a wide range of methods in educational research. Experienced researchers tend to find the descriptions of methods rather superficial and, in some cases dated, but new researchers can do worse than use this book as an initial source for finding out what is meant by basic terms and for locating some key references.

WALFORD, G. (Ed) (1991) *Doing Educational Research*, London: Routledge. In this book thirteen researchers describe and reflect upon their experiences of carrying out particular research projects. Although none of their studies directly concerned literacy the researchers' accounts of the struggles and choices which they encountered provide insights into what research is about. Issues of 'method' are placed in a more realistic context.

Chapter 7

Literacy in Professional Development

Overview

Previous chapters have reflected on literacy as a social and political phenomenon, as an activity which people in the past engaged in differently from those today, as an activity certain to change in the future, as a matter of individual development, as something to be taught and as an object of research. In each of these there is a sense in which the discussion has been about other people's literacy, that is people other than readers of this book. Now I want to bring the discussion nearer home by reflecting on aspects of literacy likely to experienced by a majority of readers of this book – teachers taking Masters' courses in education. I wish to focus on two aspects of academic literacy which may be somewhat new to teachers studying at this level – research writing and literature searching. More attention will be given to the former than to the latter. There are other aspects of academic literacy which can be new to Masters' students (e.g. critical reading of research reports, writing proposals, writing up observations, skim reading abstracts) but focusing on these two will, I hope, be sufficient to show some characteristics of literacy practices and at the same time, by highlighting some practical issues, to make it easier to engage in them.

Research Writing

An important component of Masters' level work is carrying out a research study – albeit a small scale one appropriate for the time available for a dissertation or project assignment. Writing is indispensable to doing research firstly because research can hardly be said to be completed until it is written up. Unwritten research is unfinished research. It is difficult to see how an activity can count as research at all if it is not shared with other people in a form which enables them to understand it critically. A helpful definition of research, from Lawrence Stenhouse (1981), is that it is 'systematic enquiry made public'. Being systematic and making research public involves writing. Even if findings are disseminated through videos, posters or performance some writing is usually necessary. Conventionally, the medium for dissemination is the *research report*, whether this takes the form of a research article, a book, a thesis or a dissertation. A dissertation completed as part of an MEd course is something *written* and it is also usually *public* in that generally a copy is placed in a university library and will be available to others.

The quality of research writing can either enhance or undermine the value of a piece of research. Sometimes such writing poses difficulties for students. That is one reason to focus on it here. However, as this book concerns literacy, there are additional reasons for being interested in this particular kind of writing. It is desirable to be as aware of this form of literacy in our own work as we are of other forms of literacy in the lives of our students. I want to draw attention to two key aspects of research writing – the *process* of doing it and the nature of the *product* itself – and to make some specific remarks about dissertations. First, however, it is necessary to clarify the place of writing in research.

The Importance of Writing in Research

Writing is most obviously important as the *end point* of research. For Masters' students this includes the dissertation but there are other kinds of end point research writing such as the following.

Professional journal articles
Research journal articles
Chapters
Books
PhD theses
Texts for oral presentations
Posters
Video scripts
Popular accounts (in newspapers, magazines)
Press releases

Although not all these forms of writing are required on Masters' courses, they are employed to varying extents by researchers in literacy and it is quite possible that readers may engage in them one day themselves. Writing is also often necessary for *securing research opportunities*, for example in letters seeking permission or cooperation in studying in schools or other organisations, in research proposals, and in applications for funding or course admission.

More important perhaps is *writing as a research tool*. Many examples can be given of this.

Field notes – e.g. in an ethnographic study
Observations – e.g. in studying tutor strategies
Transcription – producing a written record from an audio-tape
Instruments – interview schedules, questionnaires, checklists
Personal journals – notes on one's developing thinking
Working papers – for limited circulation
Drafts for 'end point' writing

A particularly interesting use of writing as a research tool is in developing one's thinking. This can be in notes in a personal journal or it can be in any of the other forms of writing. The sociologist Howard Becker (1986), in his *Writing for Social Scientists: How to Start and Finish your Thesis, Book or Article*, explains how writing can shape a researcher's thinking:

> First one thing, then another, comes into your head. By the time you have the fourth thought, the first one is gone. For all you know, the fifth thought is the same as the first . . . You need to give the thoughts a physical embodiment, to put them down on paper. A thought written down (and not immediately thrown into the wastebasket) is stubborn, doesn't change its shape, can be compared with the other thoughts that come after it. (Becker, 1986, p. 55)

Lucy McCormick Calkins (1986) uses the metaphor of a 'lens' to describe how writing out one's thoughts can help clarify them:

> Halfway down the page, I realize that a puzzling contradiction has emerged. I reread what I have written, re-seeing what I have said; the writing becomes a lens. I revise, and by moving the words on the page and looking through them at my unfolding subject, I explore, and discover what I have to say. (Calkins, 1986, p. 17)

Looking at the many different ways in which writing enters research can be very revealing. It becomes clear that writing is not just the end point of research or something that one does along the way. Rather, the activity of research is revealed as essentially a *writing activity*, albeit one which has to be integrated into other activities too such as talking, looking, and thinking.

Although curiosity and enquiry are natural human activities, doing research may not come naturally and can be difficult. Part of the difficulty consists – to return to Stenhouse's terms – in making one's enquiry systematic *and* public through writing. There are two ways in which we can try to become better writers – whatever our stage of development. One is to attend to the *process* of writing and how it can be facilitated; the other is to try to understand better what we are aiming to produce, the *product*.

Research Writing as Process

The activity of writing can be viewed as a process in which there a number of stages. For example, Graves (1984) has used the terms 'pre-composing', 'composing' and 'post-composing'. Murray (1985) and Calkins (1986) talk of 'rehearsal', 'drafting', 'revision' and 'editing'. It is acknowledged that stages need not follow in a fixed order, that one stage can merge into another, and that writers may circle back through some stages.

The identification and description of stages and their order results from theorists reflecting on their own writing process and their observations of other writers writing particular kinds of texts. It follows therefore that the descriptions will vary according to one's own writing style, the groups of writers observed (e.g.

children, college students, professional writers), and what is being written (fiction, correspondence, research reports). We have to be wary of too definite statements of the writing process when there are so many variables and the fundamental processes cannot be observed directly. Nevertheless, by combining logic, introspection, anecdote and observation we can construct a reasonable description of the process which can help us see ways of improving it.

I suggest that reflection on the writing process can be considered in terms of these five stages.

1   Pre-composing
2   Drafting
3   Revising
4   Editing
5   Sharing

The better we understand these stages, the more likely it is that we can find ways to make our writing easier and more effective.

It is very important to recognise that the writing process begins well before one sets pen to paper or fingers to keyboard. In the *pre-composing* stage writers take the decision to write something and form the intention of communicating something to one or more readers. It is vital to recognise the social nature of this stage. Our reasons for writing, as well as the decisions made about what needs to be written, in what order, and for whom, are all shaped by the group we belong too, whether that is a group of friends, a family, an educational institution, a research community or a popular readership. Of course some writing is private (e.g. a diary or a personal research journal) but, even then, what is written is probably shaped by the writer's social relations with others.

In some writing the pre-composing stage may be fairly short or even instantaneous but, in research, pre-composing can take – sometimes *should* take – a long time. It is in this stage that one first finds words to express what is to be communicated (words which one may or may not continue to use until the final writing up of the study). In the case of writing a dissertation, the pre-composing stage could include the first informal conversations with colleagues, supervisor, friends or family about what is to be researched. The way a study is constructed at this stage – the very words and phrases used – will influence the rest of the writing process.

In the pre-composing stage there needs to be some clarification of the purpose of what is to be written, the audience, the genre to be used, the scale of the writing (100 words or 15,000?), and how it can be structured. Noting down ideas, producing outlines, refining key phrases can help in this stage. There can therefore be some writing in the pre-composing stage, even if it is not quite the kind of writing which is being aimed at for the final product.

Sooner or later, one has to get on with the writing proper – the composing of text. It is helpful to refer to this as *drafting* since many writers at this stage recognise that what they will produce can be very rough – the important thing being to get something down on paper. This stage – like all the others in the writing process – involves the *formation of ideas*. Drafting can mean exploring and playing with ways of expressing ideas. It can clarify and change what we think in the manner described by Becker and Calkins quoted earlier.

As soon as there is a draft, writers can move into the stage of *revision*. Some writers prefer to get all their ideas down on paper as quickly as possible knowing that, as it will be revised later, the quality of their first draft is unimportant. They may write hundreds or even thousands of words before they start to revise their text. Other writers find it difficult to draft more than a few words without beginning to revise what they have just written. Others revise as they write *and* at the end. The draft–revise–redraft cycles vary in scale and speed but there is no reason for preferring any one approach to the another provided the writer is satisfied with the final result. What is important to recognise is that revision of drafts is an indispensable part of good writing. If we admire a piece of writing it is very likely that the writer has laboured over many drafts. The eighteenth century writer, Samuel Johnson remarked, 'What is written without effort is in general read without pleasure'. J.K. Galbraith, well known for the quality of his writing on economics and society, said, 'the note of spontaneity that my critics say they admire so much appears only in the fifth draft' (Galbraith, 1993, p. vii).

What can be said about how to revise drafts? Much will depend on individual taste but the points made in the box may be worth bearing in mind.

There are perhaps two key ideas in these suggestions. One is *structure* – having the right structure, sticking to it, and making it apparent to the reader through 'signposts' such as headings, subheadings and key words. Writers have a responsibility to be clear in their message as a whole as well as in the individual words and sentences which make it up. A second idea is *brevity*. The writer's aim should be to have readers engage with ideas rather than with words. The fewer words used to convey an idea, the easier it will be for the reader to grasp it.

Naturally, revision takes time. This is something for which new writers may be unprepared. Yet if they do not allow time for revision, they may have to settle for an inferior result. It can – paradoxically – be time consuming to achieve brevity. The French philosopher Pascal once apologised in a letter to a friend, 'I am sorry this is such a long letter – I didn't have time to write a shorter one.' Most writing tasks are time-limited by some kind of deadline (something which students writing assignments and lecturers writing teaching materials know only too well). Therefore we have to make compromises and recognise the

> **Some questions to consider in revising drafts**
>
> Do I have the right structure for the document?
> Does the order of ideas reflect the structure?
> Can I make the structure more explicit (e.g. through headings/ subheadings, paragraphing, opening /closing sentences, key terms)?
> Am I using any unnecessary terms or jargon?
> Can I say the same in fewer words?
> Have I engaged/interested the reader?

need to finish a piece of writing even though more time could make it better. The point is to be aware that there *is* a trade-off, and to reconcile the opposing pressures of time and quality according to the demands being faced.

After drafting and revising, comes *editing* (see box). This refers to the final presentation of a piece of writing in the form expected (or required) by readers. It requires an understanding of genre (to be discussed later).

The last stage in writing is *sharing*, by which is meant giving it to one or more readers. This can take many forms ranging from showing a piece of writing to a friend, submitting a report to one's supervisor or to publishing a book. It is the final act necessary for all research writing (although not, of course, for purely personal writing). For many writers this can be an anxious stage. There is a certain risk in exposing our work to others' scrutiny, especially if we are likely to experience criticism of what we write as criticism of *us*. This can lead to delay in finishing a writing task but we have to recognise that a part of writing is, to use Becker's (1986) phrase, 'getting it out the door.' It may help to give a piece of writing first to an audience that is likely to be sympathetic. Finally, an interesting aspect of sharing, and the feedback from readers, is that it can begin the pre-composing stage for a future piece of writing.

Having looked at the five stages of pre-composing, drafting, revising, editing and sharing, let us consider how this description of the writing process can be used to identify ways in which it can be made easier or more effective. Those who experience no difficulty with writing, and are entirely satisfied with what they produce, need read no further. The rest of us, however, may find it worthwhile to reflect on how we currently handle the five stages and how we could handle each of them differently in the future. For example, do we try to skip the first stage of pre-composing and go straight into writing? If so, we may be making the drafting stage harder (and eventually much longer) than it needs to be. It might be worth thinking about ways of enhancing the pre-composing stage, for example by taking opportunities to talk about ideas at an early stage or by keeping an 'ideas notebook'. Other stages can be reviewed in a similar way. If it is hard to start drafting, would a 'warm up' spell of a few minutes' free writing help? In drafting, it is worth checking whether sufficient time is allowed for 'playing' with ideas and exploring alternative formulations. In revising, perhaps we could have other people look at our drafts in exchange for us doing the same for them? In relation to editing, do we really know the appropriate conventions? In relation to sharing, do we accept and, if necessary, do we contrive opportunities for showing other people our writing (or do we shrink from such opportunities)? The more writing writers do, the more they

> **Some questions to consider in editing**
>
> Have I got (and do I understand) *all* the formal requirements for the document?
> Citations and references – complete?
> Have I got the most effective page layout (including spaces) and character fonts?
> Have all spelling mistakes and 'typos' been removed?

realise that there are options at each stage. If one approach is unsuccessful, there is often another.

Research Writing as Product

Accounts of the writing process are incomplete if they do not also consider what it is that the writer is trying to produce. All writing – apart from the purely personal – has to be understood in relation to *genre*. Either it conforms to some genre or it has to be understood as a deliberate variation or violation of well understood genres.

The concept of 'genre' is not easy to define but it has proved useful in linguistic and literacy studies. According to Webster's Dictionary a genre is 'a distinctive type or category of literary composition'. The term is often applied to types of film, music or painting. In linguistics it can be defined in very elaborate terms but Swales (1990) defines it generally as 'a distinctive category of discourse of any type, spoken or written, with or without literary aspirations' (p. 33).

There is a social dimension to genre. Distinctive categories of discourse arise as a way of 'doing business' within particular communities. Thus, in oral discourse in Britain there are widely understood genres of greeting, requesting information, communicating news on TV, beginning and ending seminars, and so on. In other countries, communities may manage such things differently. In written discourse, there are widely understood ways of writing letters, newspaper reports, course prospectuses, and so on. Each of these can be considered genres and behind every genre, shaping it, is a community of some kind.

In research there are genres of writing shaped by the community of researchers. Examples are:

> Research articles
> Abstracts
> Research proposals
> Dissertations/theses
> Titles of books, articles, dissertations
> Posters

For example, if we look at the genre of *research articles* in journals it is apparent that they can be distinguished from other texts by such features as titles, abstracts, sections, headings/subheadings, citations, references, page layout and conformity to journal style. They often have some less obvious features such as titles which follow a certain structure (e.g. the accessible 'phrase-colon-description' such as 'What no bedtime story means: narrative skills at home and in school'), abstracts which 'sell' the article, introductions which follow a predictable structure, statistics, tables, quotations and acknowledgements. Every genre, and each feature of a genre, represents an agreed way in which a community – in this case the research community – manages its affairs.

What does this mean for writers, especially new writers? It means that understanding research writing – learning how to do it better – is about social understanding as well as acquiring writing skills in a narrower sense. This sort of understanding is difficult to teach directly – not least because members of the research community have not developed an explicit understanding of it themselves.

For example, the practice of citing previous research in an article could have many social purposes: to indicate sources of evidence; to enable readers to check details of context or procedures; to acknowledge others' intellectual property; to pay homage (nods all round to previous researchers); to operate a co-operative reward system ('you cite me, I'll cite you'); to do what is conventionally expected; to increase chances of an article being accepted by a journal; for rhetoric (to give air of authority); to offer evidence for admission to a discourse community; to creation of a personal research space. Some of these purposes are respectable; others less so. Yet they may all influence this feature of research writing.

Literacy research can deepen our understanding of research writing genres. For example, Swales (1990) investigated how the introductions to research articles were structured. From an analysis of many such introductions he concluded that there were three things which authors sought to do in the introductions to their articles, and that there were only a limited number of ways they could do each. He described what had to be done in terms of three 'moves':

1   Establishing a 'research territory' (explaining to the reader what area of research the article concerns, and where in that field the author's research is situated).
2   Establishing a 'niche' (explaining the nature of the author's contribution to the field).
3   'Occupying the niche' (previewing the main points of that contribution).

Swales (1990) referred to this as the CARS (Creating A Research Space) model. He attempted to identify the various ways in which writers could make these three moves as follows.

Move 1   Establishing a territory
      Claiming centrality
      and/or Making topic generalisation(s)
      and/or Reviewing items of previous research
Move 2   Establishing a niche
      Counter-claiming
      or Indicating a gap
      or Question-raising
      or Continuing a tradition
Move 3   Occupying the niche
      Outlining purposes
      or Announcing present research

Announcing principal findings
Indicating structure of article

Can this understanding of research genres help writers? It cannot be a 'how to do it' formula to be followed but it may be helpful in indicating that there are features of the research writing genre of which one can usefully be aware. Some features are explicit, others implicit. Understanding them is a matter of recognising the inevitability of genre in discourse communities and trying to identify the characteristics of those genres one wants to engage in (or challenge) in one's own writing.

Writing a Dissertation

This takes us to the *dissertation genre*. What are the characteristics of this genre, what is needed for a good dissertation, and how can the process of writing a dissertation be facilitated?

A Master's level dissertation can be seen as having four essential characteristics. First, it is an account or report of *research*. Often that research will be empirical – involving the collection and analysis of data of some kind – but there are other kinds of research. Some (e.g. textual or historical or philosophical studies or research reviews) can be done in a library whereas empirical studies require work in colleges, schools, communities or other field settings. Second, there must be something *original* about the research. This is not as hard to achieve as it may sound for it does not mean that the entire study has to be *completely* original. What matters is that the researcher is bringing something new to a topic. This means that using other researchers' methods is acceptable (indeed, that is often desirable) and attempting to replicate previous researchers' findings can be valuable. Third, a dissertation reports a *substantial* piece of work. This is difficult to quantify but, depending upon course regulations, as a rough guide one could think of a dissertation as equivalent, say, to the work needed for all the other course work or some proportion of the course work. This means several weeks of full time study or a longer period of part time study. Fourth, it is vital that the dissertation research is *linked to previous research* in the field. It must build on previous work in some way – perhaps by extending existing lines of research, filling in gaps or challenging existing understandings. This means a good literature review into which the dissertation study can be contextualised. Students sometimes feel that no research has been done into the topic which interests them but this is nearly always because they have defined the topic too narrowly or failed to see how research in other fields is linked to it (or because they have not carried out an adequate literature review).

These four characteristics – research, originality, substance, links to previous research – are necessary for a research report to be accepted as a Master's level dissertation but this still leaves enormous scope for individual variation. Also, there are other characteristics which, while not necessary, are certainly typical of many dissertations. For example, a large number of dissertations will concern practical questions facing teachers or tutors and will contribute directly to the development of practice. Others will have a professional benefit in terms of preparing a tutor or teacher for a new area of work in their future careers.

Dissertations also have some structural characteristics which may be regarded as conventional ways of achieving various purposes within the genre. Some of these are spelt out in regulations and course documentation (e.g. layout, size of paper, having an abstract, references, page numbering, binding). Other characteristics of the genre are implicit. Dissertations need titles, conventionally more than two or three words but rarely more than twenty. They are usually organised into numbered sections or chapters. They may have appendices. A typical structure includes:

> Title page
> Abstract (around 100 words)
> Contents page listing chapters, diagrams, tables
> Chapter giving a short introduction/description of the topic
> One or two chapters reviewing previous work in the field
> A chapter explaining how the writer's research relates to previous research, the research questions/aims, and the methods used in the research
> One or two or more chapters detailing findings
> A chapter discussing the significance of the findings and the adequacy of the research study
> A short conclusions chapter
> References
> Appendices

Obviously, some studies (e.g. biographies, personal reflections) may require a different structure. The above is one to be considered, adapted or rejected as appropriate. Some writers may have good reasons for challenging the conventional structure but they still need to think about how their dissertation satisfies the fundamental characteristics of the genre.

So much for product, what about the process of writing a dissertation? Here we can refer to the five-stage model offered earlier and reflect on how each stage can best be managed. For example, to facilitate the pre-composing stage, many courses provide early opportunities to think, write and talk about topics in order to clarify interests and thinking. As this stage proceeds it may be helpful to have a provisional dissertation outline, indicating possible chapters and their content. It is advisable to have a 'word budget' for different chapters in order to break down the writing task and to avoid the common mistake of writing too much. In relation to the other stages, one can reflect upon the approaches one has developed in the past and ask whether it is worth modifying any of them for writing a dissertation. When will you start drafting? Who can you show drafts to? How many drafts can you afford to revise? In editing, are you clear about the formal requirements for dissertations? What opportunities can you take or contrive for sharing your writing before, during, and after the course? By applying such simple ideas – some derived from literacy research – the ways in which one writes, and the quality of what is written, can be enhanced.

Literature Searching

Another aspect of academic literacy which may be new to teachers on Masters' courses is having to use university libraries and search the research literature on some topic. They may well have had years of experience of libraries – in childhood, as undergraduate students, and as adult users – but this may have involved little more than finding specific items through library catalogues or simple browsing. Masters' courses, with their emphasis on research and independent study, require a more sophisticated use of libraries. Increasingly, this is a matter of electronic literacy too. It is important to understand the potential of modern libraries – both those found in universities and local libraries. We can reflect on this as a form of literacy and analyse how to acquire it using concepts discussed in Chapter 4 on literacy development, i.e. in terms of becoming engaged in a social practice as well as developing certain skills.

There are three reasons why it is worth thinking carefully about literature searching, libraries and how to get the most out of them in professional development. First, as professionals, teachers should know how to locate and retrieve information and ideas relevant to their field of work. Second, teachers of literacy will find it easier to teach their pupils or students how to use libraries and find information – a significant aspect of contemporary literacy – if they are themselves confident and effective library users. Third, as Masters' students, there will be occasions when teachers' studies will be more interesting and worthwhile if they can go beyond the materials provided through the course. This becomes vital at the dissertation level.

Using libraries is partly a matter of understanding the nature of the services available and how they can help achieve professional objectives. Therefore teachers – whether or not they are Masters' students – need technical information about how to use libraries to which they have access. But library use is also a matter of understanding one's own attitudes to libraries and information retrieval, and being clear about what libraries mean in professional terms. An important part of studying for a degree – particularly a postgraduate degree – is using a library to read around topics, to prepare for assignments, and generally to learn from the past and current work of other teachers and researchers across the world whom we could never meet in person but who have written about matters which concern us.

Teachers who never use a library have less opportunity for interesting and worthwhile study. The ambition should be to go beyond merely covering materials provided by courses. For example the National Literacy Strategy in England provides extensive training materials for primary school teachers. These materials (however excellently selected, edited, written, presented and so on) suffer from one great disadvantage. They emanate from one source, in this case a government department. If teachers wish to go further, to evaluate them critically, to consider alternatives, to challenge ideas or explore new areas they will have to make use of libraries. If they are studying on courses, particularly if they are doing dissertations, libraries are even more important.

Becoming a Competent Literature Searcher

To acquire any form of literacy some sense of its function and meaning is important. What, then, can be gained by becoming a competent library user?

A good university library will be a storehouse of texts, some of which will be highly relevant to students' studies. Most obviously there are books and many libraries still describe themselves in terms of the number of books they contain. In addition there will be copies of journals with issues of past volumes bound as books. But libraries have always been more than the books they store. They are also windows into a wider – indeed a world-wide – store of texts. Items contained in one library can be used to identify items held elsewhere and, through inter-library loan arrangements, users of one library can often obtain copies of relevant items not stored in their own library. At postgraduate level this is crucially important for, if they are working anywhere near the edge of existing knowledge, students cannot expect to find everything they may need at their own university's library. Electronic databases, usually accessed via the internet, are now the most common and most powerful means of identifying relevant material. Since these can be accessed through computers beyond the library building itself, and since the texts so identified can sometimes be sent electronically to users, the concept of a library is undergoing radical redefinition. One can imagine 'virtual' libraries in the future – not confined to particular places or buildings and not clearly distinguishable from other internet information sources. That day, however, has not yet arrived. Most texts in education required by Masters' students (books, journal articles, reports) are still being printed on paper and the archives of such material produced and stored in the past remain extensive. Also, libraries are places where librarians work and can most easily provide support for users. Libraries are therefore likely to be sites of academic study for many years to come.

Becoming a competent library user means being familiar with details of the literacy practices involved. Many of these are matters of convention or are arbitrary. They include mundane details of physical accessibility, layout, opening hours and so on as well as the logic of cataloguing systems and a vocabularly of special terms (e.g. monographs, serials, bibliography, book stacks, Dewey system). There are parallels here with young children's initial literacy development which has to include coming to terms with conventions such as letters, letter names, left-to-right reading, punctuation and so on. These conventions are not what literacy is really about but not knowing them means that more meaningful activity is impossible.

A basic activity in library use is finding relevant material. One way to do this is to look it up in the catalogue by author or title. But suppose you do not know what to look up – that you first need to find out what is available on a given topic? Some people like to browse along shelves where there are other books on the topic or on related topics. This can be interesting but it is a very inefficient way of searching for material. If books are out on loan or shelved under another classification number they will never be found. One can use a catalogue to see what books a library has at a given subject classification (e.g. on the Dewey classification system many books on literacy topics are at 374 and adjacent numbers) or see what books there are for particular keywords (most computerised library catalogue systems have this facility). This is still a limited way of searching because it is limited to books, and to books held at a particular library. There may be relevant material in a book held at another library or it may be in an article in a journal or a chapter in a book. To find such material a better search strategy is needed.

The first step in a search strategy is to define one's topic as clearly as possible. Sometimes this means recognising that it is actually two or three topics which may require separate searches. The definition of a topic can be expected to change as one reads more of the literature but some key terms are needed to get started. These can be used in electronic searches of library catalogues and the major educational research databases such as the Educational Resources Indexing Center (ERIC) and the British Educational Index (BEI) to yield a set of potentially relevant sources. They can also be helpful in trawling through print-based sources in libraries such as card catalogues, encyclopedias, bibliographies, periodical indexes, periodicals abstracts, report literature, research in progress, theses and dissertations, government publications, statistics, conference proceedings and newspapers. A good search strategy has to be tailored to the time available and to how important it is to find *all* the relevant material. For example, it would be surprising if many students working on, say, a 5,000-word assignment could spend more than a few hours searching for (as opposed to *using*) material. For a dissertation, however, the equivalent of several days' searching the literature would be more appropriate; for a PhD study one needs to think in terms of weeks or months. Further inspection of abstracts and the documents themselves is necessary to weed out those which are totally irrelevant or only marginally relevant. Bibliographies (lists of publications on a topic) which turn up in a search can be particularly useful. At the same time informal search techniques can be used. For example, one usually knows at the outset of certain books, articles or reports which are central to the topic. They can be examined for references to relevant literature. The same thing can be done with the contents pages of key journals in a field. This is sometimes the only way of tracking down items such as chapters in books which may not be listed in databases or indices. The names of key authors in a field can be used to track down their other publications. Informal techniques can be combined with formal ones. For example, if one knows that a certain article is central to the search topic one can check what key terms have been used to describe it in databases and ensure that these descriptors are used in the formal searches. There is no reason why informal techniques should not include asking other people (supervisors, fellow students, colleagues) for leads to follow up. Also, serendipity has a part to play. Once embarked on a clearly defined search it is interesting how often one comes across relevant items (e.g. in newspapers, in conversations, in bookshop browsing) without deliberately searching them out. Chance favours the prepared mind.

As the activity of literature searching is examined it becomes apparent that it is an excellent example of a literacy practice. We can see how it requires those who engage in it to have certain skills (to use a library catalogue, to access databases, to file references, and so on) but these skills are not exercised by individuals working in isolation. They are part of a social practice in which reading and writing activities, supported by oral language, are integrated into the activity of a larger group – in this case the educational research community. Learning to use libraries and carry out a literature search, like learning to write for research purposes, is about joining a community.

Further Reading

BECKER, H.S. (1986) *Writing for Social Scientists: How to Start and Finish your Thesis, Book or Article*, Chicago: University of Chicago Press. In this engaging and practically oriented minded book the sociologist Howard Becker addresses many of the concerns of students new to research writing. In fact it is hard to conceive of writers of any level not finding something of interest and value in it.

SWALES, J.M. (1990) *Genre Analysis: English in Academic and Research Settings*, Cambridge: Cambridge University Press. Swales was one the first to attempt to characterise the genre of research writing. Although his findings and analyses have subsequently been challenged by other researchers this book remains an accessible and interesting introduction to the issues.

Chapter 8

Reflecting on the Context for Reflection

Overview

In this concluding chapter I want to discuss the context within which teachers of literacy – whether on Masters' courses or not – and researchers have to work. This context shapes the way we think about literacy, it generates problems and issues for research, it determines what opportunities there are for professional development and for doing research, and it sets the parameters by which research may affect policy and practice. The main contextual features of which we need to be aware are national policies regarding literacy in education, regarding educational research and regarding professional development for teachers and tutors. The aim of the chapter is to encourage critical awareness of each of these, with particular reference to England where the current policy context emphasises actions over reflection, rather than a balance between the two.

What Would be the Ideal Context?

To assess the current context, and whether it could be more conducive to reflection, it helps to have some idea about what would be desirable. The actual can then be compared to the desirable. There will be different opinions on this, of course, since one person's view of what is desirable may not be the same as another's. Also, it is rare for literacy educators and researchers to express clear views of what they think should be done overall at national level. They generally find it easier to advocate specific measures in their specialist field or to criticise details of policy than to say what national policy should be since that involves deciding what political goals are priorities and what action is feasible and likely to attain them.

In 1996, however, with a general election in the UK imminent, the National Literacy Trust did invite literacy organisations and certain individuals in the field to offer views on what policy should be. Contributors were allowed 1,200 words to state their perspectives and advice on the strategic agenda for literacy over the next five years. Thirty-six contributions were published in a book titled, *Building a Literate Nation* (McClelland and National Literary Trust, 1997) just weeks before the election which brought a new Labour government into power. It is revealing to see how the contributors responded to the challenge of having to say what should be done. Many appeared reluctant or unable to address issues beyond their specialist interests. Perhaps they were not used to reflecting on strategic national policy which, of course, must be developed as a coherent whole rather than an aggregate of separate actions. Several contributors did accept the challenge at that level and what they say makes interesting reading in the light of subsequent developments. It could be a valuable exercise for all literacy educators periodically to produce 1,200 words on such a topic.

As one illustration of what this might involve I offer my own contribution to *Building a Literate Nation* (Hannon, 1997) below. I argued that a strategic agenda for literacy depends on understanding our current situation, deciding on key goals and identifying methods likely to achieve them.

In line with the arguments in Chapter 1, I began by accepting that there *is* a literacy problem. The ability to use written language is as vital as ever to learning, to a productive life, and to full citizenship. In education it remains central at every stage from reception class to further or higher education. The problem is not at the upper end of the achievement range where there are many effective and confident users of written language but in the huge variation in achievement and the 'long tail' at the lower end. There are too many children whose restricted literacy denies them access to the curriculum and who leave school with minimal qualifications. They enter a society with 'no place to hide' in using written language. Too many adults have literacy difficulties which prevent them finding employment or retraining for new jobs.

A national strategy has further problems to address. Many teachers and tutors, vital for policies to raise literacy have in recent years been demotivated, undervalued and deskilled by past policy which has been driven by a distrust of professionals and an emphasis on teacher-proof solutions which bypass teachers' thinking. Opportunities for professional development have been restricted to training in how to implement centrally determined programmes. Teachers and tutors struggle with a shortage of resources – textbooks, school libraries and public libraries.

There are some features of the current policy context which need to be kept in mind. We are in a confusing period of rapid, technologically driven change. 'On-screen literacy' requires altered reading and writing skills and is opening up new ways in which written language can satisfy basic communicative and expressive purposes. 'Print literacy', too, is being changed by technology – particularly in the interrelationships between image and word. There are implications for how we conceptualise and measure achievement and underachievement. Another current feature is that literacy has become an ideological battleground. Many claims about the problem and how to solve it are not just about literacy. They have to be understood on an ideological plane too. For example, saying that workforce literacy levels are too low for international economic competitiveness is both a claim about literacy *and* a claim about determinants of national economic performance – in particular about the causes of unemployment. Such claims may direct attention away from other economic factors such as investment policies, employers' needs for a pool of unemployed workers, low public expenditure on education, and so on. Also, the adverse effects of persistent poverty or family unemployment on educational achievement are not problems which can be tackled only by changing the teaching of literacy. Many groups have an interest in certain ways of framing, exaggerating or minimising problems or in urging certain solutions. All claims about the current literacy problem therefore have to be read critically. There are also, however, some positive features in the current situation. They include the high level of interest in literacy, across a wide range of groups; the UK still being one of the most literate in the world; increasing multilingualism; and most citizens being native speakers of one of the most widely used world languages.

I suggested that there should be four key goals for literacy policy in the years to come.

1   *Reducing low achievement in primary education.* This phase must be the priority since the longer children are allowed to fall behind, the harder it is for them to catch up, and the greater the waste of resources. Overall levels of achievement should be raised by reducing the 'tail'. Action can be before school entry and in the early years of schooling.
2   *Developing an effective range of 'catch-up' programmes.* These are needed at all stages to enable children falling behind to be identified and helped. Reading Recovery is only one example; there need to be many more, targeted at different categories of learners at different ages.
3   *Expanding 'return to learning' choices.* These are needed for the many who have already left school and for those beyond the reach of programme in the school years. Choice means literacy learning opportunities available in different settings – workplace, community, further education – for different ethnic and age groups.
4   *Integrating research into policy formation.* Research can enable us to refine methods and obtain better value for money from different programmes. We need more than prejudice, fashion and ideology to develop effective policy.

What should be the methods for achieving these goals? My own suggestions included the following.

1   Increasing resourcing per pupil in primary education to level of secondary and using the extra for literacy.
2   Developing a *range* of remedial approaches rather than relying on 'one shot' solutions.
3   Changing funding arrangements for adult education and further education (FE) to encourage provision of a wider range of post-school literacy learning opportunities.
4   Energising teachers – making them part of the solution, not part of the problem.
5   Involving parents, starting early, and recognising more than one model of family literacy.

6   Increasing local responsibility, decreasing central control.

7   Ending the pretence that lack of resources is no problem even if they cannot be increased immediately – particularly important in relation to compensatory programmes.

8   Being open to new forms of literacy, not trying resist the tide of new technology redefining what it means to be literate.

9   Getting back to basics (of which the most fundamental are learners understanding what purposes written language can serve for them and how they can acquire it), not focusing on skills to the exclusion of purposes, keeping in mind the fundamental purposes of education, and fostering critical literacy from the start.

10 Establishing literacy as a main strand of a national educational research programme, using central government funds to stimulate/steer a national research strategy in partnership with universities and research sponsors.

11 Resisting temptation to present non-literacy problems as literacy problems.

12 Thinking long term, having a sense of urgency but acting as if there is a future beyond the next parliamentary session. Ending cynical, short term public relations gimmicks.

Government, I argued, should start by saying, 'There is a literacy problem. We haven't got all the answers but we are going to mobilise people to tackle it.' Government should take some initiatives centrally but concentrate on returning responsibility – and accountability – to those who have to implement solutions, and give them the tools to do the job.

I do not claim that the above reflections and suggestions about policy have special merit or that they deserve priority over those of my fellow citizens whose views may be different but I do claim that stating one's views is a precondition for having a dialogue with others and for developing a critical appreciation of current national policy. If your priorities and methods are different from mine, what are they and why do you think they are better? I might learn from yours. Dialogue and debate is a democratic necessity.

Current National Policy

How does current government policy compare to the above? The government has published its policy, which it is currently implementing with great energy, in two key documents, the July 1997 White Paper, *Excellence in Schools* (DfEE, 1997) and the final report of its Literacy Task Force (1997b), *The Implementation of the National Literacy Strategy* (in August 1997). No doubt, as time goes on, policy-as-implemented will differ from the policy as originally envisaged and presented but the key points, the assumptions, the reasoning and implementation plans are there to be critiqued in the documents.

The government's priorities are different from those suggested above and by other contributors to *Building a Literate Nation*. There is certainly an emphasis on achievement in primary education but the National Literacy Strategy is more about raising standards for all children than raising the low achievement of those constituting the 'tail'. Consequently, less effort has been put into preschool literacy intervention or programmes for children having difficulties in the early years of schooling. More focused programmes would mean putting significantly more resources into disadvantaged communities than into others. It is possible that low achievers will do better as a result of government policy but the distance between them and more successful children is not likely to be reduced. Regarding adults 'returning to learning', it is still too early to judge the government's commitment to expanding choices but there are signs that it does wish to promote 'lifelong learning'. As to research, there is little indication of it being used systematically for policy formation.

Current policy is very much at odds with the following suggestion from *Building a Literate Nation*.

> Energise teachers – make them part of the solution, not part of the problem. Trust them. Restore autonomy. Improve professional development opportunities. End the search for 'teacher proof' programmes. (Hannon, 1997, p. 35)

Government policy does see teachers as essential for raising literacy achievement in primary schools but the detailed prescriptions of the National Literacy Strategy have considerably restricted teacher autonomy. In the short term this may achieve government aims but the danger is that the long term consequences will be a less effective teaching force. There are curious echoes here from the beginning of the century when teachers were still shaking off the chains of our first national curriculum, the infamous 1862 Code. One educator in that period, Edmund Holmes (1911), described it thus:

> The State, in prescribing a syllabus which was to be followed ... by all the schools in the country, without regard to local or personal considerations, was guilty of one capital offence. It did all his [*sic*] thinking for the teacher. It told him in precise detail what he was to do each year in each 'Standard', how he was to handle each subject, and how far to go in it; what width of ground he was to cover ... In other words it provided him with his ideals, his general conceptions, his more immediate aims, his schemes of work; and if it did not control his methods in all their details, it gave him (by implication) hints and suggestions ... on which he was not slow to act. (Holmes, 1911, pp. 104–5)

Holmes argued that in the early twentieth century this policy had proved disastrous.

> What the Department did to the teacher, it compelled him to do to the child. The teacher who is the slave of another's will cannot carry out his instructions except by making his pupils the slaves of his own will. The teacher who has been

deprived by his superiors of freedom, initiative and responsibility cannot carry out his instructions except by depriving his pupils of the same vital qualities. (Holmes, 1911, p. 104)

Holmes was not alone in thinking on these lines and the result was that government gradually passed control of curriculum and pedagogy to schools where it remained for most of the century (until government took it back in 1988 by introducing the National Curriculum). The earlier episode in the history of education, now so far beyond the reach of living memory, suggests that central control of methods of teaching literacy can have unfortunate consequences.

The Role of Research in Literacy Education

Perhaps it is unfair to compare the National Literacy Strategy to the 1862 Revised Code. It could be argued that the National Literacy Strategy will provide teachers with skills which will enable them to have genuine choice and control over their teaching. This is a researchable issue. One could study the implementation and processes of the strategy to determine its impact on teaching as well as on children but, sadly, there is at present little sign of this being investigated.

The National Literacy Strategy began in England in 1996 as the 'National Literacy Project' involving over 250 schools and hundreds of teachers. They were the first to use the new framework for teaching and to try the literacy hour with the support of consultants. It was a £14 million experiment in literacy education. One might have expected an evidence-based rationale for it but at the time none was made public. One might also have expected plans for collecting evidence about the 'experiment' even if that word can be used only in the loose sense of 'trying something new', rather than in its research sense. There was a wonderful opportunity in 1996 for comparing the 250 project schools with a control group. Ideally, a large sample of schools meeting the project criteria (low literacy standards, readiness to volunteer for a project) should have been allocated at random to project or control conditions. Any subsequent difference between the two groups could be attributed to project methods. That, essentially, is a 'true experimental design'. The underlying logic is straightforward – it is an obvious way to find out if doing X is better than doing Y – but it rarely appeals to policy makers – perhaps because they already *know* that X is better or that it is the only politically acceptable option. The Labour Party Literacy Task Force (1997a) recommended such an experimental evaluation of the National Literacy Project before the 1997 general election When the Labour government came into power the Task Force dropped the idea and the Project was 'rolled out' in 1998 to all schools as the National Literacy Strategy (Literacy Task Force, 1997b). There was still no research-based rationale although one was commissioned *later* (Beard, 1999). The National Literacy Strategy has good features, and it is helpful that the evidence-base for them is now public, but we rely for much of the evidence (including experimental studies) reviewed by Beard (1999) on other countries. In summary, research has not played as much of a role in the development and implementation of the National Literacy Strategy as one might have wished.

Turning to broader features of the research context, there has, in recent years, been considerable discussion about the health of educational research in Britain. Some critics claim that it is too remote and of too little practical relevance to teachers' needs to have much impact on education (Rudduck and McIntyre, 1998).

Research can have a 'diffuse' influence as well as a 'direct' influence. Diffuse need not mean weak or unimportant. Atmospheric oxygen is diffuse but actually quite important. No one should expect single research studies to change classroom practice or policy. When research changes practice – as it undoubtedly has done in the teaching of literacy – it is more often the cumulative effect of many researchers' work over many years. Such change can be deep – at the level of teachers' thinking – as well as in the modification of specific techniques. Teachers do not use research as a cookbook but as a resource in constructing their view of what is worth aiming for and likely ways to get it.

The problems with research into literacy in Britain cannot be addressed solely in terms of what researchers do or fail to do – the issues they study, the methods they use, the quality of their work, how they disseminate findings, and so on. These are obviously very important but they are not the whole picture. We also need to think about the wider system of which research is a part. To take an ecological metaphor, think of educational research as a living plant in interaction with its environment – constantly renewing itself, sometimes growing, sometimes declining. At present it could be healthier but we need to work out the extent of ill health and whether the causes are internal or environmental. We need to get the diagnosis right to foster healthy growth. A good gardener does not uproot or cut back a plant which fails to thrive if the real problem is choking weeds or lack of soil nutrients, pollination or sunlight.

Professional Development and Research

The teaching profession is perhaps the most important part of the ecological system in which educational research is situated and it is the weakened capacity of teachers to engage with research which is also weakening educational research. This issue takes us to the heart of the education policy of recent governments.

Teachers need a certain amount of professional autonomy to engage with research. If, as in the National Literacy Strategy, they are not free to change what they do, why should they engage with research which might show them better ways of doing it? Teacher autonomy has been severely reduced because a driving principle of government policy has been distrust of the profession. Since the implementation of the National Curriculum, teachers have had to contend with a detailed prescriptive curriculum, exhausting bureaucratic demands, and elaborate surveillance systems to ensure compliance. When this failed to deliver desired results in literacy government's response was even more specific central control.

Top-down, supposedly teacher-proof programmes are *de rigueur*. As a result, professional development for teachers is too often reduced to training them to put other people's ideas into practice. Curricular and pedagogic initiatives at the level of the school or local area are suffocated. Gone are the days of local courses, teachers' centres, active professional organisations, support for Masters' level study, and the celebration of teacher researchers. Add to this worsened working conditions relating to class sizes and the physical deterioration of schools, and rising levels of stress, and one has to ask how much attention it is reasonable to expect teachers to give to educational research. For practitioners to be engaged *with* research some should ideally be engaged *in* it, and all must have the opportunity to read, reflect upon, discuss, and act on research findings.

This is not to blame teachers for the problems of educational research but to point to factors governing the application of research which are beyond researchers' control regardless of the relevance, quality and dissemination of their work. Many practitioners are interested in research, would seek it out, and often want to undertake it – if only they had better working conditions, less stress, more freedom to act, and enough time to engage critically with it. In this area comparisons with other professions such as doctors and engineers are instructive – they appear to have greater professional autonomy and opportunities for self-directed development.

The problem is two-way. For research to be any good, it needs to be challenged and shaped by a critical response from practitioners. If practitioners are denied opportunities for a dialogue with researchers, the eventual result will be low quality research. Where is the reward or excitement for educational researchers if their only audience is other researchers? Again, an ecological perspective reveals how health inside the educational research community is linked to that outside.

This takes us to an urgent issue in professional development where universities can make a powerful and unique contribution – how teachers can be enabled to engage with research. Professional development has other important purposes too, such as skill development, but, because universities have a unique role in research sharing it with practitioners deserves their special attention. Educational research is virtually useless if it cannot be shared with educators.

From this point of view, the quality of educational research depends upon practitioners being able to engage with it. Without that, educational researchers are reduced merely to doing research, and reporting it, for each other.

Let us imagine the ideal form of professional development for literacy educators to engage with research. It would involve some kind of group experience – a course perhaps – in the company of other teachers, where there would be guidance and support (preferably from active researchers) in critically examining research, discussing it, reflecting on it, relating it to theory and practice. There would be opportunities to write about these things. There would be access to a well stocked library containing relevant books and journals and perhaps guided internet access to the wider store of research in international databases. There would be opportunities to undertake small scale research to get that insider awareness of research which can only come from doing it oneself. There might also be opportunities to get involved in larger scale research with others. This would be a platform for those who wished to go on to more sustained studies of their own.

This ideal already exists. It is a description of a Master's degree in education. MEd courses were created in the 1960s and many teachers have since taken them. Despite lack of financial support in recent years, teachers continue to take Masters' courses. It is rarely in the interests of any particular school in a particular year or term, that they should fund a member of staff on a long course. Local education authorities, under pressure to deliver short term targets, and with very limited resources, are also unlikely to support teachers' engagement with research. In the current context, such professional development is likely to be viewed as an alternative, dispensable activity compared to literacy teaching. Individual teachers have seen it differently and have committed their own resources in it but this is a poor way for Britain to develop educational research or teachers' ability to use it. Education nationally has needs which are not the same as those of individual schools or areas.

We should strive for an *entitlement* for educators, if they so wish, to spend some of their time, at least once in their careers, in Masters' study or some other collaboration with a university. Reflection on literacy in education, aided by research, is not an alternative to literacy education but a necessary means for ensuring its effectiveness and value.

Further Reading

McClelland, N. (Ed) (1997) *Building a Literate Nation: The Strategic Agenda for Literacy Over the Next Five Years*, Stoke-on-Trent: Trentham Books. This book collects together the thirty-six responses to the 1996 National Literacy Trust invitation to literacy organisations and some individuals to offer their 1,200-word 'perspectives and advice on the strategic agenda for literacy over the next five years'. It is worth reading both as a snapshot of views about literacy at the end of the twentieth century and as a basis for reviewing governmental policy as it actually developed.

Rudduck, J., and McIntyre, D. (Eds) (1998) *Challenges for Educational Research*, London: Paul Chapman Publishing/Sage. Following criticisms directed at educational research in the mid-1990s, this book brings together reflections by sixteen British educational researchers on key issues which have to be faced. Like the *Building a Literate Nation* collection, this one assembles views about educational research, the role of practitioners in it, and its relevance to both practice and policy.

References

ADAMS, M.J. (1990) *Beginning to Read: Thinking and Learning about Print*, Cambridge, MA: MIT Press.

ADULT LITERACY AND BASIC SKILLS UNIT (ALBSU) (1987) *Literacy, Numeracy and Adults: Evidence from the National Child Development Study*, London: Adult Literacy and Basic Skills Unit.

APPLE, M.W. (1986) *Teachers and Texts: A Political Economy of Class and Gender Relations in education*, New York: Routledge and Kegan Paul.

APPLEBEE, A.N. LANGER, J.A. and MULLIS, I.V.S. (1988) *Who Reads Best? Factors Related to Reading Achievement in Grades 3, 7 and 11*, Princeton, NJ: Educational Testing Service.

ARCHER, D. and COSTELLO, P. (1990) *Literacy and Power: The Latin American Battleground*, London: Earthscan.

ARNOLD, H. (1982) *Listening to Children Reading*, London: Hodder and Stoughton.

AUERBACH, E.R. (1995) 'Which way for family literacy: Intervention or empowerment?', in MORROW, L.M. (Ed.) *Family Literacy: Connections in Schools and Communities*, Newark, DE: International Reading Association.

BARTON, D. (1994) *Literacy: An Introduction to the Ecology of Written Language*, Oxford: Blackwell.

BARTON, D. and HAMILTON, M. (1998) *Local Literacies: Reading and Writing in One Community*, London: Routledge.

BEARD, R. (1990) *Developing Reading 3–13* (2nd edn), London: Hodder and Stoughton.

BEARD, R. (Ed) (1993) *Teaching Literacy, Balancing Perspectives*, London: Hodder and Stoughton.

BEARD, R. (1999) *National Literacy Strategy: Review of Research and Other Related Evidence*, London: Department for Education and Employment.

BECKER, H.S. (1986) *Writing for Social Scientists: How to Start and Finish your Thesis, Book or Article*, Chicago: University of Chicago Press.

BELL, J. (1993) *Doing your Research Project: A Guide for First-Time Researchers in Education and the Social Sciences*. Buckingham: Open University Press.

BIELBY, N. (1998) *How to Teach Reading: A Balanced Approach*, Leamington Spa: Scholastic.

BIRCHENOUGH, C. (1914) *History of Elementary Education in England and Wales*, London: University Tutorial Press.

BOLTER, J.D. (1990) *Writing Space*, Hillsdale, NJ: Lawrence Erlbaum.

BROOKFIELD, K. (1993) *Writing*, London: Dorling Kindersley/British Library.

BROOKS, G., FOXMAN, D. and GORMAN, T.P. (1995) *Standards in Literacy and Numeracy: 1948–1994*, London: National Commission on Education.

BROOKS, G., PUGH, A.K. and SCHAGEN, I. (1996) *Reading Performance at Nine*, Slough: National Foundation for Educational Research.

BROWN, C. (1975) *Literacy in 30 Hours: Paulo Freire's Process in North East Brazil*, London: Writers and Readers Publishing Cooperative.

BRYANT, P.E., BRADLEY, L., MACLEAN, M. and CROSSLAND, J. (1989) 'Nursery rhymes, phonological skills and reading', *Journal of Child Language*, 16, pp. 407–28.

BUSHELL, R., MILLER, A. and ROBSON, D. (1982) 'Parents as remedial teachers: An account of a paired reading project with junior school failing readers and their parents', *Journal of the Association of Educational Psychologists*, 5(9), pp. 7–13.

BYRNE, B. (1998) *The Foundation of Literacy: The Child's Acquisition of the Alphabetic Principle*, Hove: Psychology Press.

CAIRNEY, T. (1995) *Pathways to Literacy*. London: Cassell.

CALKINS, L.M. (1986) *The Art of Teaching Writing*, Portsmouth, NH: Heinemann.

CATO, V. and WHETTON, C. (1991) *An Enquiry into Local Education Authority Evidence on Standards of Reading of Seven-Year-Old Children: A Report by the NFER*, London: Department of Education and Science.

CENTRAL ADVISORY COUNCIL FOR EDUCATION (England) (1967) *Children and their Primary Schools* (Plowden Report), London: HMSO.

CHALL, J. (1983) *Stages of Reading Development*, New York: McGraw-Hill.

COHEN, L. and MANION, L. (1994) *Research Methods in Education* (4th edn), London: Routledge.

COMMISSION OF THE EUROPEAN COMMUNITIES (1988) *Report on the Fight against Illiteracy. Social Europe, Supplement 2/88*, Luxembourg: Office for Official Publications of the European Communities.

DANIELS, H. (Ed) (1993) *Charting the Agenda: Educational Activity after Vygotsky*, London: Routledge.

DAVIE, R., BUTLER, N. and GOLDSTEIN, H. (1972) *From Birth to Seven: A Report of the National Child Development Study*, London: Longman/National Children's Bureau.

DAVIES, A. and RITCHIE, D. (1998) *THRASS Teacher's Manual*, Chester: THRASS (Teaching Handwriting Reading and Spelling Skills).

DELGADO-GAITAN, C. (1990) *Literacy for Empowerment: The Role of Parents in Children's Education*, London: Falmer Press

DEPARTMENT FOR EDUCATION AND EMPLOYMENT (1997) *Excellence in Schools* (White Paper, Cm 3681), London: The Stationery Office.

DEPARTMENT FOR EDUCATION AND EMPLOYMENT (1998) *The National Literacy Strategy: Framework for Teaching*, London: DfEE.

DEPARTMENT OF EDUCATION AND SCIENCE (1975) *A Language for Life* (Bullock Report), London: HMSO.

DEPARTMENT OF EDUCATION AND SCIENCE (1990) *The Teaching and Learning of Reading in Primary Schools*, London: DES.

DONALDSON, M. (1978) *Children's Minds*, Glasgow: Fontana/Collins.

DONALDSON, M. (1993) 'Sense and sensibility: Some thoughts on the teaching of literacy', in BEARD, R. (Ed) *Teaching Literacy, Balancing Perspectives*, London: Hodder and Stoughton.

DOUGLAS, J.W.B. (1964) *The Home and the School: A Study of Ability and Attainment in the Primary School*, London: MacGibbon and Kee.

EISENSTEIN, E.L. (1982) *The Printing Press as an Agent of Change: Communications and Cultural Transformations in Early-Modern Europe*, Cambridge: Cambridge University Press.

EKINSMYTH, C. and BYNNER, J. (1994) *The Basic Skills of Young Adults: Some Findings from the 1970 British Cohort Study*, London: Adult Literacy and Basic Skills Unit.

FERREIRO, E. and TEBEROSKY, A. (1982) *Literacy before Schooling*, Portsmouth, NH: Heinemann.

FOGELMAN, K. and GOLDSTEIN, H. (1976) 'Social factors associated with changes in educational attainment', *Educational Studies*, **2**, pp. 95–109.

FREIRE, P. (1970) *The Pedagogy of the Oppressed*, trans. Myra Bergman Ramos, Harmondsworth: Penguin.

FREIRE, P. (1972) *Cultural Action for Freedom*, Harmondsworth: Penguin.

FRITH, U. (1985) 'Beneath the surface of developmental dyslexia', in PATTERSON, K.E., MARSHALL, J.C., and COLTHEART, M. (Eds) *Surface Dyslexia*, London: Lawrence Earlbaum.

GALBRAITH, J.K. (1993) *The Culture of Contentment*, Harmondsworth: Penguin.

GARTON, A. and PRATT, C. (1998) *Learning to be Literate: The Development of Spoken and Written Language* (2nd edn), Oxford: Blackwell.

GEE, J.P. (1996) *Social Linguistics and Literacies: Ideology in Discourses* (2nd edn), London: Falmer Press.

GIBBON, E. (1896) *The History of the Decline and Fall of the Roman Empire*, London: Methuen (original work published 1776).

GOELMAN, H., OBERG, A.A., and SMITH, F. (Eds.) (1984) *Awakening to Literacy*, Portsmouth, NH: Heinemann.

GOODMAN, K. (1969) 'Analysis of oral reading miscues: Applied psycholinguistics', *Reading Research Quarterly*, **5**(1), pp. 9–30.

GOODMAN, Y.M. (1986) 'Children coming to know literacy', in TEALE, W.H. and SULZBY, E. (Eds) *Emergent Literacy: Writing and Reading*, Norwood, NJ: Ablex.

GOODMAN, Y.M. (Ed) (1990a) *How Children Construct Literacy: Piagetian Perspectives*, Newark, DE: International Reading Association.

GOODMAN, Y.M. (1990b) 'Children's knowledge about literacy development: An afterword', in GOODMAN, Y.M. (Ed) *How Children Construct Literacy: Piagetian Perspectives*, Newark, DE: International Reading Association.

GOODMAN, Y.M. (1997) 'Multiple roads to literacy', in TAYLOR, D. (Ed) *Many Families, Many Literacies: An International Declaration of Principles*, Portsmouth, NH: Heinemann.

GOSWAMI, U. (1999) 'Phonological development and reading by analogy: Epilinguistic and metalinguistic issues', in OAKHILL, J. and BEARD, R. (Eds) *Reading Development and the Teaching of Reading: A Psychological Perspective*, Oxford: Blackwell.

GOSWAMI, U. and BRYANT, P. (1990) *Phonological Skills and Learning to Read*, Hove: Lawrence Erlbaum.

GRAFF, H. (1979) *The Literacy Myth: Cultural Integration and Social Structure in the Nineteenth Century*, New Brunswick, NJ: Transaction.

GRAFF, H. (1987) *The Labyrinths of Literacy*, Lewes: Falmer Press.

GRAVES, D. (1984) *A Researcher Learns to Write*, Exeter, NH: Heinemann.

HALL, N. (1987) *The Emergence of Literacy*, London: Hodder and Stoughton.

HANNON, P. (1987) 'A study of the effects of parental involvement in the teaching of reading on children's reading test performance', *British Journal of Educational Psychology*, **57**, pp. 56–72.

HANNON, P. (1995) *Literacy, Home and School*, London: Falmer Press.

HANNON, P. (1997) 'Achieving key goals', in MCCLELLAND, N. and NATIONAL LITERACY TRUST (Eds) *Building a Literate Nation: The Strategic Agenda for Literacy Over the Next Five Years*, Stoke-on-Trent: Trentham Books.

HANNON, P. (2000) 'Rhetoric and research in family literacy', *British Educational Research Journal*, **25**(5), pp. 121–38.

HANNON, P. and JACKSON, A. (1987) *The Belfield Reading Project Final Report*, London/Rochdale: National Children's Bureau/Belfield Community Council.

HANNON, P. and NUTBROWN, C. (1997) 'Teachers' use of a conceptual framework for early literacy education involving parents', *Teacher Development*, **1**(3), pp. 405–20.

HANNON, P. and WOOLER, S. (1985) 'Psychology and educational computing', in WELLINGTON, J.J. (Ed) *Children, Computers and the Curriculum*, London: Croom Helm.

HANNON, P., WEINBERGER, J. and NUTBROWN, C. (1991) 'A study of work with parents to promote early literacy development', *Research Papers in Education*, **6**(2), pp. 77–97.

HAVELOCK, E. (1982) *The Literate Revolution in Greece and its Cultural Consequences*, Princeton, NJ: Princeton University Press.

HEATH, S.B. (1982) 'What no bedtime story means: Narrative skills at home and school', *Language in Society*, **11**(2), pp. 49–76.

HEATH, S.B. (1983) *Ways with Words: Language, Life and Work in Communities and Classrooms*, Cambridge: Cambridge University Press.

HEWISON, J. and TIZARD, J. (1980) 'Parental involvement and reading attainment', *British Journal of Educational Psychology*, **50**, pp. 209–15.

HOLMES, E. (1911) *What Is and What Might Be*, London: Constable.

HURRY, J. (1999) 'Annotation: Children's reading levels', *Journal of Child Psychology and Psychiatry*, **40**(2), pp. 143–50.

JAMES, W. (1960) *The Varieties of Religious Experience* (The Gifford Lectures delivered at Edinburgh, 1901–2), London: Fontana.

JEAN, G. (1992) *Writing: The Story of Alphabets and Scripts*, London: Thames and Hudson.

JOHNSTON, P. H. (1985) 'Understanding reading disability: a case study approach', *Harvard Educational Review*, **55**(2), pp. 153–77.

KIRSCH, I.S., JUNGEBLUT, A., JENKINS, L. and KOLSTAD, A. (1993) *Executive Summary from 'Adult Literacy in America': A First Look at the Results of the National Adult Literacy Survey*, September, Princeton, NJ: Educational Testing Service.

KOHL, H. (1974) *Reading, How To*, Harmondsworth: Penguin.

LANDOW, G.P. (1992) *Hypertext: The Convergence of Contemporary Critical Theory and Technology*, Baltimore, MD: Johns Hopkins University Press.

LANKSHEAR, C. (1987) *Literacy, Schooling and Revolution*, Lewes: Falmer Press.

LINDSAY, G., EVANS, A. and JONES, B. (1985) 'Paired Reading versus Relaxed Reading: A comparison', *British Journal of Educational Psychology*, **55**, pp. 304–9.

LITERACY TASK FORCE (1997a) *A Reading Revolution: How We Can Teach Every Child to Read Well: The Preliminary Report of the Literacy Task Force*, London: Literacy Task Force.

LITERACY TASK FORCE (1997b) *The Implementation of the National Literacy Strategy*, London: Department for Education and Employment.

LLOYD, S. (1998) *The Phonics Handbook* (3rd edn), Chigwell: Jolly Learning.

MACCABE, C. (1998) 'End of the word?', *Guardian, Screen*, 10 July, p. 14.

McCLELLAND, N. and NATIONAL LITERACY TRUST (Eds) (1997) *Building a Literate Nation: The Strategic Agenda for Literacy Over the Next Five Years*, Stoke-on-Trent: Trentham Books.

McGUINNESS, C. and McGUINNESS, G. (1998) *Reading Reflex: The Foolproof Method for Teaching your Child to Read*, Harmondsworth: Penguin.

McGuinness, D. (1998) *Why Children Can't Read and What We Can Do about It*, Harmondsworth: Penguin.

McLuhan, H.M. (1962) *Gutenberg Galaxy: The Making of Typographic Man*, Toronto: University of Toronto Press.

Manguel, A. (1996) *A History of Reading*, London: Flamingo.

Meek, M. (1982) *Learning to Read*, London: The Bodley Head.

Meek, M. (1988) *How Texts Teach What Readers Learn*, Stroud: Thimble Press.

Michael, I. (1993) 'Seventeenth century teachers' views on reading and spelling', in Brooks, G., Pugh, A.K. and Hall, N. (Eds) *Further Studies in the History of Reading*, Widnes: United Kingdom Reading Association.

Millard, E. (1997) *Differently Literate: Boys, Girls and the Schooling of Literacy*, London: Falmer Press.

Miskin, R. (1997) *Best Practice Phonics*, London: Heinemann.

Moser, C. (1999) Interviewed on BBC Radio 4 *Today* programme, 24 March.

Murray, D. (1985) *A Writer Teaches Writing* (2nd edn), Boston, MA: Houghton Mifflin.

Nation, K. and Hulme, C. (1997) 'Phoneme segmentation, not onset-rime segmentation, predicts early reading and spelling skills', *Reading Research Quarterly*, 32, pp. 154–67.

Nelson, T. (1987) *Literary Machines*, edition 87.1. [Quoted and cited in Tuman, 1992, p. 55.]

Neuman, S.B. and McCormick, S. (Eds) (1995) *Single-Subject Experimental Research: Applications for Literacy*, Newark, DE: International Reading Association.

Neuman, S.B. and Roskos, K.A. (1998) *Children Achieving: Best Practices in Early Literacy*, Newark, DE: International Reading Association.

Newson, J. and Newson, E. (1977) *Perspectives on School at Seven Years Old*, London: Allen and Unwin.

Olson, D. (1994) *The World on Paper*, Cambridge: Cambridge University Press.

Parlett, M. and Hamilton, D. (1977) 'Evaluation as illumination: a new approach to the study of innovatory programmes', in Hamilton, D., Jenkins, D, King, C., MacDonald, B. and Parlett, M. (Eds) *Beyond the Numbers Game: A Reader in Educational Evaluation*, London: Macmillan.

Piaget, J. and Inhelder, B. (1969) *The Psychology of the Child*, London: Routledge and Kegan Paul.

Pinker, S. (1998) Foreword to McGuinness, D., *Why Children Can't Read and What We Can Do About It*, Harmondsworth: Penguin.

Postman, N. (1970) 'The politics of reading', *Harvard Educational Review*, 40(2), pp. 244–52.

Pressley, M. (1998) *Reading Instruction that Works: The Case for Balanced Teaching*, New York: Guilford Press.

Radical Statistics Education Group (1982) *Reading Between the Numbers: A Critical Guide to Educational Research*, London: British Society for Social Responsibility in Science.

Reid, J. (1993) 'Reading and spoken language: The nature of the links', in Beard, R. (Ed) *Teaching Literacy, Balancing Perspectives*, London: Hodder and Stoughton.

Reinking, D. (1994) *Electronic Literacy: Perspectives in Reading Research No. 4*, Universities of Georgia and Maryland: National Reading Research Center.

Reinking, D., McKenna, M.C., Labbo, L. and Kieffer, R.D. (Eds) (1998) *Handbook of Literacy and Technology: Transformations in the Post-Typographic World*, London: Lawrence Erlbaum.

ROBINSON, A. (1995) *The Story of Writing: Alphabets, Hieroglyphs and Pictograms*, London: Thames and Hudson.

ROBINSON, P. (1997) *Literacy, Numeracy and Economic Performance*, London: Centre for Economic Performance, London School of Economics and Political Science.

RUDDUCK, J. and MCINTYRE, D. (Eds) (1998) *Challenges for Educational Research*, London: Paul Chapman Publishing/Sage.

SIMON, B. (1960) *Studies in the History of Education, 1780–1870*, London: Lawrence and Wishart.

SIMON, B. (Ed) (1972) *The Radical Tradition in Education in Britain*, London: Lawrence and Wishart.

SMITH, F. (1988) *Joining the Literacy Club*, Portsmouth, NH: Heinemann.

SNOW, C. (1991) 'The theoretical basis for relationships between language and literacy in development', *Journal of Research in Childhood Education*, 6(1), pp. 5–10.

STENHOUSE, L. (1981) 'What counts as research?' *British Journal of Educational Studies*, 29(2), pp. 103–14.

STREET, B. (1984) *Literacy in Theory and Practice*, Cambridge: Cambridge University Press.

STREET, B. (1995) *Adult Literacy in the United Kingdom: A History of Research and Practice*, NCAL Technical Report TR95-05, Philadelphia, PA: National Center on Adult Literacy.

SWALES, J.M. (1990) *Genre Analysis: English in Academic and Research Settings*, Cambridge: Cambridge University Press.

TAFT, M. (1991) *Reading and the Mental Lexicon*, Hillsdale, NJ: Lawrence Erlbaum.

TAYLOR, D. (1997) 'Preamble', in TAYLOR, D. (Ed) *Many Families, Many Literacies: An International Declaration of Principles*, Portsmouth, NH: Heinemann.

TEALE, W.H. and SULZBY, E. (Eds) (1986) *Emergent Literacy: Writing and Reading*, Norwood, NJ: Ablex.

THORNDIKE, R.L. and HAGEN, E.P. (1969) *Measurement and Evaluation in Psychology and Education*, New York: Wiley.

TIZARD, B. (1993) 'Early influences on literacy', in BEARD, R. (Ed) *Teaching Literacy, Balancing Perspectives*, London: Hodder and Stoughton.

TIZARD, B., BLATCHFORD, P., BURKE, J., FARQUHAR, C. and PLEWIS, I. (1988) *Young Children at School in the Inner City*, London: Lawrence Erlbaum.

TIZARD, J., SCHOFIELD, W.N. and HEWISON, J. (1982) 'Collaboration between teachers and parents in assisting children's reading', *British Journal of Educational Psychology*, 52, pp. 1–15.

TOPPING, K.J. (1997) 'Electronic literacy in school and home: A look into the Future', *Reading Online. http: //www.readingonline.org/international/future/index.html*

TOPPING, K.J. and LINDSAY, G. (1991) 'The structure and development of the paired reading technique', *Journal of Research in Reading*, 15(2), pp. 120–36.

TUMAN, M. (1992) *Word Perfect: Literacy in the Computer Age*, London: Falmer Press.

UNDERWOOD, G. and BATT, V. (1996) *Reading and Understanding*, Oxford: Blackwell.

UNESCO (1988) *1990: International Literacy Year (ILY)*, ED/ILY/88.10, Paris: UNESCO.

VYGOTSKY, L.S. (1962) *Thought and Language*, Cambridge, MA: MIT Press.

VYGOTSKY, L.S. (1978) *Mind in Society: The Development of Higher Psychological Processes*, Cambridge, MA: Harvard University Press.

VYGOTSKY, L.S. (1986) *Thought and Language*, Cambridge, MA: MIT Press.

WALFORD, G. (Ed) (1991) *Doing Educational Research*, London: Routledge.

WALKER, C. (1975) *Teaching Prereading Skills*, London: Ward Lock Educational.

WEBSTER, A., BEVERIDGE, M. and REED, M. (1996) *Managing the Literacy Curriculum: How Schools Can Become Communities of Readers and Writers*, London: Routledge.

WEDGE, P. and PROSSER, H. (1973) *Born to Fail?*, London: Arrow Books/National Children's Bureau.

WELLS, G. (1985) 'Pre-school literacy-related activities and success in school', in OLSON, D.R., TORRANCE, N. and HILDYARD, A. (Eds) *Literacy, Language and Learning*, Cambridge: Cambridge University Press.

WELLS, G. (1987) *The Meaning Makers: Children Learning Language and Using Language to Learn.* London: Hodder and Stoughton.

WITTGENSTEIN, L. (1953) *Philosophical Investigations*, Oxford: Blackwell.

WORKING GROUP ON POST-SCHOOL BASIC SKILLS (1999) *A Fresh Start: Improving Literacy and Numeracy* (Moser Report), London: Department for Education and Employment.

WRAGG, E.C., WRAGG, C.M., HAYNES, G.S. and CHAMBERLIN, R.P. (1988) *Improving Literacy in the Primary Schools*, London: Routledge.

Author Index

Subject Index